✠

The Order of Dionysis and Paul
A Brief Historical & Spiritual Overview

On Monday, the 19th of July 1948, the idea of forming a Psycho-Physical Healing Group was put to the members of the Meditation Group who had been meeting at the Bristol Quest Club for over a year.

A brief summary of the work and ideals involved had been prepared for them to read and they agreed unanimously that it was a splendid idea.

Two members mentioned that they had been feeling for some time that the Meditation Group might do some such work, although nothing definite had formed in their minds.

Each contributed some money to be used for advertising etc. and this was collected by Mr. Jones, as Treasurer for the Meditation Group.

It was agreed to break away from the Quest Club and to hold future meetings at 2, Etloe Road.

Signed

Dennis Green

Rev. D. Ph.D. D.D. D.Py.

Frontis.   Photocopy of 'Notice'.

The Order of Dionysis & Paul

A Brief Historical & Spiritual Overview

✠

by

Allan Armstrong ODP

With an Introduction by

Dr. R. A. Gilbert

ODP Publications

BRISTOL 2018

First published in 2018 by
ODP Publications,
an imprint of Imagier Publishing
United Kingdom

Email: ip@imagier.co.uk
www.imagier.co.uk

ISBN: 978-1-910216-28-6

Cover and text design by Allan Armstrong
with material supplied by Sr Claudia

The paper used in this publication is from a
sustainable source and is elemental chlorine free.

Printed and bound in Great Britain by 4Edge Ltd.

Contents

Illustrations

Acknowledgements

It is a matter of fact that in writing this book I have accumulated numerous debts of gratitude that cannot go unmentioned. In particular, I owe a great deal of thanks to Dr R A Gilbert for his dedicating so much time to scrutinising the raw text, and for writing the introduction; although not a member, he has known the Order for longer than anyone I can think of.

I am also grateful to Sr Claudia for her time and patience in reading the text and listening to my thoughts, and who frequently stimulated my thinking in conversation, and for her contribution of photographs and paintings *et al*. I am also indebted to Brother Luke, whose enthusiastic interest was especially important in the Winter of 2017, and to Sister Sophia, whose encouragement and proof-reading was especially useful.

I should also like to acknowledge that I have relied extensively upon the Order Records as my source of information concerning almost all that is referred to herein, supported by Peter Anson's book, *Bishops at Large*, (London, Faber & Faber, 1964) with additional references from personal sources, memories and reflections.

Last but not least, I give thanks to my wife and children for their tolerance and encouragement, and to my extended Christian family of brothers and sisters following the Path.

Allan Armstrong
The Chapel of St Raphael
Wiltshire 2018

Preface

This book is not so much a history of events, or a record of what has happened to the Order laid out in a chronological line, but a story of a transformation from one state to another very different state. The reader will note that the pathway is chronological in that there is necessarily a given timeline, following the pageant of key events that have shaped the Order. But it is also a story of rebirth that exists simultaneously outside and within space-time.

It exists outside of space-time, in that it concerns the invisible development and emergence of a spiritual essence taking place within the heart and mind of the Order. Yet, it clearly exists within space-time, as described in the Order's record of that emergence; not all of which is comfortable. With hindsight it is possible to see that what has happened to the Order over the years needed to happen – that there were no accidents or mishaps, only opportunities to grow and to learn – comfort is then a matter of perspective!

Our civilisation has been subject to a thousand-year rule of Logic and a four-hundred year rule of Reason. The benefits of which need not be discussed here. However, as I write, the world is clearly in deep trouble because the lessons we need to learn concerning, self-control, tolerance, patience, kindness, sharing, land and financial reform etc, although identified by logic and reason, are not issues they are designed to deal with. They are spiritual problems requiring spiritual remedies that are not readily found within the parameters of the rational world.

Religion has been the traditional means by which we are able to find the answers to such problems. Unfortunately, it too has succumbed to the *force majeure* of logic and reason. Arguably, since the turn of the eighteenth century, reason rather than inspiration has been the primary method of acquiring insight into the mysteries of religion. This is a problem the world over, because reason at best, can only explain this world it knows, and frequently fails to do even that. In truth, the more rational religion has become, the more impotent it has grown. By comparison, those religions that are by definition non-rational, have thrived.

The primitive Church had been shown a pathway by the Lord that led its people from the bestial state they had been born into, towards a state of spiritual enlightenment. These two states are described as the first and second Adam (1 Corinthian 15: 31-51). In the first three centuries catechumens were taught to walk this pathway before they were baptised. The path may have been mysterious, but it was nonetheless a real, present and personal experience. After Constantine, the Church slowly lost sight of this precious jewel, and by the end of the first millennium started to rely more on logic than inspiration. The result is there for all to see, a divided Church depending primarily upon reason to educate its flock, yet relying upon a literal interpretation of countless 'reasonable' versions of the Scriptures to show them the way forward.

The Order of Dionysis & Paul (ODP) makes no claim to perfection, for after all that may be said and done, the notion of achieving human perfection is, generally speaking, little more than an unachievable ideal in this world. However, spiritual perfection, embodied in our exemplar, the Lord Jesus Christ, is another matter; concerning which, the members of the Order do follow that Path to the best of their ability. This brief history of the ODP is not only about its emergence and evolution in this world, but also, and more importantly, it is about the Path and how it goes before the Order as "a pillar of fire by night and a pillar of smoke by day." Those who know of what I speak will know that I speak openly and truthfully. In the words of Meister Eckhart:

> *"There is an agent in my soul which is perfectly sensitive to God. I am as sure of this as I am that I am alive."*
> *Sermons 6.*

Introduction

For reasons that are geographical, rather than religious, I have been aware of – and later involved with – the Order of Dionysis and Paul, and the Church within which it grew, for the greater part of my life.

I was born in Bristol and grew up close to Dennis Green's old home – and even closer to the Church of the Three Magi, where I first met him. While I was busy buying a bull-roarer with my pocket money, my father held a long conversation with Fr Green – almost certainly about esoteric matters, for my father was both a stage magician and a keen psychical researcher. He was also the source of my own later fascination with the occult.

Seven years later, in 1962, I made my first real acquaintance with Dennis Green when I began to attend his weekly discussion group at the little church on Ashley Hill. We debated almost every aspect of Western esotericism, and I set off on a frantic course of reading about magic, kabbalah and mysticism, with forays into Tibetan religious doctrines and practices (Dennis always said 'Tibetian').

Being young and possessed of all the superior wisdom of the brash novice, I, of course, knew everything and corrected everyone. They in turn, being patient, kind and knowledgeable soon set me aright, although over time I began to realise that it was not Dennis, but Morris Saville who truly and deeply understood the content and meaning of the Western Mysteries.

Of the Church itself I was never a member, although I was present at the ceremonial deconsecration of the Ashley Hill chapel in 1965 and helped in the move to Pilning and in the remodelling of the church there. Perhaps because of this I was awarded a rather splendid certificate showing that I was an 'associate member', with no real obligations and free to demit at any time. My most abiding memory of that period is of a wild ride on the pillion of Morris's scooter. He had trouble in starting the engine, hung on grimly when the scooter ran away with him and fell into a ditch with it. After hauling him out I continued the ride, only to discover on reaching home that Morris had been driving blind – scarcely able to see through his mud plastered spectacles.

Not long after this, when I had fallen away from involvement with the Church, I was appointed by Mar Georgius, for reasons best known to himself, as his Consul in Bristol. It was a short-lived consulate and my duties seemed to consist only of a desultory correspondence with Mar Seraphim. At this point my connection with the Church and the Order might have ended, but Morris remained a friend, and when I lived near his flat in Cotham Brow I used regularly to walk across to it, to play chess badly (we were evenly unskilled) and to discuss esoteric topics in a far more rewarding way. Further reconnection came when my wife and I opened our bookshop (The Wise Owl Bookshop) in central Bristol. Into the shop came Allan Armstrong, and our subsequent joint history is set out in part in the later chapters of this book.

Thus far my personal role in the pre-history of the ODP, but as this book is about the Order and not about me, I should now turn a dispassionate eye upon the Order.

It is, as I perceive it, a rare and successful hybrid of a modernised Celtic Christianity and a sensitively balanced Esoteric Order. Of its Christian commitment there can be no doubt, but it is not the Church for me. I am a lifelong Anglican, of high church persuasion, but with sympathy and tolerance for other branches of the Christian faith. If I have a specific personal mission, it is to bring occultists (for want of a better term) to an awareness, understanding and acceptance of Jesus Christ, and to encourage confessing Christians to recognise that Western Esotericism

Introduction

contains within it 'jewels which the world could not afford to miss'.[1] To this end I have worked with Allan (Brother Marcus) in organising conferences, seminars and study days without either of us intruding upon the spiritual practices or theological stance of the other.

Has this been of mutual benefit? I like to think so. He has written articles and reviews for the journal I edit and has published my introductory book on Gnosticism[2]. In return I have gladly supplied introductions to such of his books as I feel qualified to do so. For me this is ecumenism in practice.

The Order of Dionysis and Paul does not exist simply for its own benefit; it is the working heart of a small Christian Church that has found a successful *modus vivendi* and will certainly continue to thrive. The same can, I trust, be said of my Church, although national Churches, by their very nature, have far larger problems. But both Churches are branches of the same tree: the Church of Christ that we shall not see fully and with absolute clarity until we finally enter the Kingdom of God.

Robert A. Gilbert
Tickenham, North Somerset,
April 2018

---

1   These are the words of C.H. Spurgeon, a noted Baptist preacher of the Victorian era. He was referring, in his book Commenting and Commentaries (1876), to material in the Jewish Talmud, Targums and Midrash.

2   *Gnosticism and Gnosis,* an Introduction (Antioch Papers, 2011)

The Beginning of
The Order of Dionysis & Paul

When did the Order of Dionysis & Paul begin? It is an intriguing question that I have often thought about over the years. When I asked my teacher, Mar Francis, about its beginnings he seemed at the time to be enigmatic. I thought he was just being playfully vague about its origins, but as I grew in the work I began to see that the question was more complex than I imagined. To understand the answer really meant understanding what the Order of Dionysis & Paul is, and when you have done that, then more than one answer comes to mind.

For example, the Order of Dionysis & Paul is a vehicle of the Holy Spirit that changes its form from time to time, but never changes its work, which is the redemption of the soul of humankind. Another answer is, it is an initiatory Order that enables people who are ready to evolve spiritually. Or, it is a vehicle for developing an esoteric understanding of Man, the Universe and God. Or, it is a religious Order within the Holy Celtic Church. All of these may be true, yet, in some ways they are incomplete. Finally, the Order of Dionysis & Paul is a precious flower in the jungle of life! Purple prose? Perhaps, but it is true and I shall try to explain what I mean by it.

According to some, we are born, we suffer and we die! A grim, even hopeless perspective, yet it is true in a limited sort of way. It is a materialistic answer to the purpose of life, which clearly tells us nothing about that purpose from a spiritual perspective. On these terms, the only benefits acquired from life are by using our minds to master Creation, and our hearts to explore what we call Love. In these two fields we spend most if not all of our lives as both slave and master. We are slave to our appetites, our dreams, our desires and our aspirations, and we are also the master of the same, or at least we could be if we were able to control our appetites, dreams, desires and aspirations – a glorious ambition that many seek but few ever achieve, and it is the purpose of the Order to unite these modes into a whole, and to sublimate their activity.

Why? Well, we appear to consist of two contrary natures. One is a good guy and the other is not. One is reliable and trustworthy, who will get up in the morning and go to work. The other is unreliable, untrustworthy, and will not get up and go to work if at all possible. One is selfish the other is generous, one is peaceful the other is aggressive, with survival at the highest level possible appearing to be the prime objective, and we never really know which one will dominate the day. From the earliest times these two parts of human nature have been recognised and incorporated into the fabric and structure of society. Some of the earliest written material known to civilisation has dealt with them in ways that we can understand today. From the *Epic of Gilgamesh* to the *Bhagavad Gita* and the *Upanishads*, from the *Pyramid Texts* of ancient Egypt to the *Edda* of the Teuton, from Genesis, the first book of the *Bible* to 1 Corinthians, in the *New Testament*, indeed, wherever we look we find the dual natures of Man described, and invariably they are described in conflict. How these two natures interact is the stuff of religion, myth and legend, and we could discuss different views about them for ever, but our purpose is to look at the question, "when did the Order of Dionysis and Paul begin?"

If the Order is a vehicle for the Holy Spirit to redeem the soul of mankind, then we could say without stretching the point too far, that it began when we were ejected from Paradise. But that doesn't really answer the question, does it? If we think of the Order as a unique entity then we are entitled to think of it having a unique beginning, and 1948 is as good a time as any. If we think of the Order as a manifestation of a spiritual need fermenting within the soul of mankind, then we can see it having many beginnings that are determined, either by culture, location or creed. On these terms the Order is a phenomenon that emerges wherever, and whenever the time is right, responding to those souls emerging from the cocoon of mortal life in need of guidance.

What strings an Order together, as on a golden chain, is 'tradition', and the tradition of the Order stretches from beyond ancient Egypt through the Graeco-Roman world down to our time. As such it nurtures those who are hungry for a truth bigger than creed or philosophy, yet accessible to those who are born into a given creed or philosophy. No person or culture has a monopoly on truth or upon God, but every culture has a way of expressing itself and its spirituality within a set of parameters, not just in the big picture but in the detail. There are of course, Orders in other cultures that speak the same truths yet use different parameters. This is right and proper, just as the Order of Dionysis and Paul today is right for its time and place.

What seems appropriate right now, was in all probability inappropriate yesterday, and may not be appropriate tomorrow; the form changes according to circumstances. The energies will take upon themselves different emphases but the essence will remain the same – the evolution and maturation of the soul. Ritual is without doubt important in such Orders, yet, without a context and a change in *habitus*, the rituals will be almost meaningless. On that note, what the Order was before 1939 gradually lost its context after 1945. As the context changed, so the *habitus* changed and so the Order needed to change. Thus, new shoots began to emerge, and in the form of a 'new shoot', the earliest written evidence concerning the beginnings of the Order of Dionysis & Paul is dated 1948. It is a notice, presumably penned by Dennis Green, the signatory. It states:

> *"On Monday the 19ᵗʰ July 1948, the idea of forming a Psycho-Physical Healing Group was put to the members of the meditation Group who had been meeting at the Bristol Quest Club for over a year.*
>
> *A brief summary of the work and ideals involved had been prepared for them to read and they agreed unanimously that it was a splendid idea.*
>
> *Two members mentioned that they had been feeling for some time that the Meditation Group might do some such work, although nothing definite had formed in their minds.*

*Each contributed some money to be used for advertising
etc. and this was collected by Mr. Jones, as Treasurer for
the Meditation Group.*

*It was agreed to break away from the Quest Club and
to hold further meetings at 2, Etloe Road.*

Signed Rev. Dr. Dennis Green."

From this notice[1] I conclude that there was a group of people who
had met for meditation at the Bristol Quest Club. How many
were in this group will probably remain unknown, although
it is unlikely to have been many more than a dozen or so, and
it is possible, even probable, that some of its members, other
than Dennis, also belonged to the Hermes Temple of the Stella
Matutina.

The notice declares that they had met at the Bristol Quest
Club for more than a year. This requires a little guesswork as the
dates are imprecise. However, the notice does imply a probable
beginning in the Spring of 1947, which does make sense, in
that the Second World War ended in September 1945, and the
country would have taken some time to return to order, and
because people would have also taken time to return home from
where they had been stationed. Thus, 1947 seems a good time
for new beginnings. The idea of forming a *Psycho-Physical healing
Group* was proposed. This becomes significant when we bear in
mind that after six years of atrocious warfare, there were many
people who were damaged, physically, emotionally and mentally.
I believe it is possible that Dennis and his fellows were looking
to contribute to the restoration of health of the many who were
damaged by the war.

The notice also declared that the group should break away
from the Quest Club. Why? This is an interesting question.
Perhaps the costs were too high? The truth is I do not know, and
I am yet unable to answer that question, but break away they
did. Future meetings were agreed to be held at number 2 Etloe
Road. Again the question arises Why? This clause is connected

---

1   See frontis

with the previous one and is just as puzzling. Why move at all? In all probability the answer is as simple as cost and opportunity. One thing is sure, as this publication will demonstrate, the Order of Dionysis & Paul did not emerge quickly. It grew slowly and quietly, evolving over the course of time. Yet, like all new shoots it has remained consistent with its objectives.

This book is an attempt to explain that process...

The Stella Matutina

Fig. 2. The site of the Stella Matutina Temple, Cotham Hill, Bristol

The Stella Matutina was a magical order dedicated to the dissemination of the traditional teachings of its predecessor the Hermetic Order of the Golden Dawn. However, we should be mindful that what the term 'magical order' meant at the turn of the 20th century is not necessarily what it means today, more than one hundred years later. For most people, magic was the study of the esoteric and symbolic dimensions of religion. This inevitably meant not just the Christian Religion, although it was a favourite, it also meant the study of comparative religion, and the study of Rosicrucianism, which involved Alchemical and Kabbalistic studies, especially with regard to healing.

The Golden Dawn (GD) had fragmented in 1900 when most of the London adepts rejected the autocratic rule of Samuel MacGregor Mathers, the then head of the Order, with the result that the GD divided into two new groups. Those who remained loyal to Mathers, among them E W Berridge and, later, John

William Brodie-Innes, took on the name Alpha et Omega, while the larger group, including such members as Dr Robert Felkin, A E Waite, Rev W A Ayton and W B Yeats, continued as the Golden Dawn. In 1901, in order to avoid public derision following the scandal of the Horos affair[2], they referred to the Order by the name of *Morgenrothe* (*i.e.* 'Morning Light').

Two years later the Order split again. A E Waite took over the remnants of Isis-Urania, and formed the Independent and Rectified Rite of the Golden Dawn, eventually dissolving it and founding the Fellowship of the Rosy Cross. Those members who preferred a more 'magical' path followed Dr Felkin into his Order of the Stella Matutina, which was dedicated to propagating and expanding the traditional teachings of the original Hermetic Order of the Golden Dawn. Nevertheless, it is important to understand that at that time all of the members had a deep interest in the esoteric expression of many kinds of spirituality. Most of the members were Christians with a deep interest in the esoteric expressions of Christian Spirituality; exploring the esoteric understanding of the ancient Church that for centuries had been understood to lie at the heart of Christianity. It is also interesting to note that the Stella Matutina included a significant number of clergy among its members.

That such a tradition exists has been accepted and written about by many over the centuries, and today many still do accept the possibility sufficiently enough to go in search of it. However, what the tradition looked like was then, as it is now, a matter of intense debate. It has many aspects that can be realised outside of the formal parameters of the Church, for example, it may be defined in alchemical, kabbalistic and magical terms, to name but a few. Good bad or indifferent, these are emotive terms that divide our society. For many, they are described, in the words of Dr R. A. Gilbert, as 'rejected knowledge', whereas for others they are stepping-stones that lead to 'enlightenment.'

Every man and woman 'taking the path' starts from a cultural base, a *habitus*, that has many forms, not all of which

---

2   See: Gilbert, *The Golden Dawn Scrapbook. The Rise and Fall of a Magical Order.* 1997, pp. 7-20.

are normal, and not all fit into categories that are easy for others to understand. We should therefore not be surprised that a member of a hermetic order or an alchemical society is interested in Christian Spirituality. Many who joined the Stella Matutina, arguably joined because the Church was unable to answer their questions, or was unready to engage with the subject-matter; whereas the Stella Matutina was not only prepared, but was also willing to do so. However, in truth it, too, lost itself among the many forms its members encountered.

Whatever the merits and demerits of the post-Victorian era, two World Wars in a short space of time rocked the foundations of a civilisation that had been 'absolutely sure of its purpose' and destiny; and in 1945 it needed to redefine itself. Clearly, magic, alchemy and the kabbalah were not the answer, but then again, neither is the fashionable cult of reason. Magic, alchemy and kabbalah are merely expressions of the human will seeking to deal with what it thinks it sees but does not understand. They are forms of cognitive dissonance relying on precepts and formulae to cover a lack of knowing. Whereas, reason seems more likely to destroy our world than save it; neither approach is sufficient. Both have their uses, but neither provide clear answers to the main questions of life such as land and monetary reform, disease, famine, war, population control and slavery. A fusion of the two might provide the answers mankind seeks, but that may also be an assumption too far. Bearing this in mind, we can understand why in the aftermath of a second great war within twenty-five years, humanity needed to redefine itself.

Dennis Green

Dennis Green was born in Bristol 1904 and died in Thornbury 1971. Of his formative years we know almost nothing. The little I have found is that he lived in the Bristol area for all of his life. He married Esmé Strong, in November 1927. Esmé was born in Bristol on 31 January 1906. They had three children, Peter, Joan and Michael. Dennis was a draughtsman working at the Bristol

Fig. 3. Rev Dennis Green

Aeroplane Company, at least before and during the 1939-45 War. At some point in the 1960's Dennis and Esmé separated, and in due course she emigrated (early 1970's) to Australia where she died. As yet we do not know the date of her death.

I understand that they were both members of the Hermes Temple of the Stella Matutina in Bristol. Dennis for fifteen years or so, demitting I believe around 1948-49. Esmé's membership details are unknown. That the Stella Matutina was an order dedicated to propagating the traditional teachings of the earlier Hermetic Order of the Golden Dawn has already been stated, but interestingly, it included a significant number of clergy among its members.

The Reverend Gerard Decieco, one of Dennis' students, and arguably his successor, destroyed most of his papers and diaries in the early 1970's. Why he did so remains a puzzle. It is understandable that he would follow Dennis' instructions and destroy papers that might be relevant to the Hermes Temple – that was his duty! Indeed, Mrs Foden, one of the last chiefs of the Hermes Temple, destroyed most of its records when it closed in the 1970's. However, to destroy everything of Dennis' writings, his diaries, his letters and other such writings is, to say the least, frustrating.

Consequently, any evidence concerning Dennis' life, the dates of his membership of the Hermes Temple, when he joined, what rank he attained and when he left, are now a matter of conjecture. However, Dr R A Gilbert, the foremost historian of the Golden Dawn, clearly recalls several members he had spoken with in the early 1970's – Mrs Foden, Ronald Huckman and his wife – acknowledging Dennis as a member. Concerning the question, 'when was he a member?' Dr Gilbert reports that the information he acquired from 'surviving members' during the 1960's and 70's suggests he was a member well into the 1950's but probably not before the War. However, the information is unclear about the pre-war period, as Dennis' stories about Carnegie Dickson suggest a pre-war membership. My views are that he joined in the early 1930's and demitted at some time after the end of the War, possibly 1948/49. My reasons for thinking along these lines are straight-forward enough. After the War Dennis had become engaged with other interests, such as raising a family, and money was tight in post-war Britain.

As I understood it from my teacher, Fr Morris Saville, one of Dennis Green's students and a Prior of the ODP until his death in 1991, Dennis had been a member of the Hermes Temple during the 1930's. Reminiscences heard by the author, in conversation with Fr Morris, and there were many such reminiscences, mostly relate to what was taking place in the Hermes Temple during the 1930's; little of what I recall related to the 1950s. One story that stands out is that a significant number of the members of the Hermes Temple were unhappy when Israel Regardie joined in 1933. I understand the Crowley association was the main reason for their unhappiness, and a significant number would not turn up when they knew he was going to be in attendance. Such reports are inevitably hearsay, but they are suggestive.

When the Second World War began in 1939, the Hermes Temple meetings were suspended for the duration of the hostilities. Those members who were eligible to fight, would have done so and people such as Dennis, who were in reserved occupations, would have been busy with the War effort. During this lengthy pause in temple activity, his life was filled in part by long hours of work, war related efforts, and with activities at the Quest Club, which I understand was located at (22?) Aberdeen Road, Bristol.

The Quest Club

Fig. 4. The Quest Club, (No. 22?) Aberdeen Road, Bristol

The Quest Club was a regular point of contact for many of those who had an interest in esoteric subjects; being frequented by the members of the Hermes Temple, Anthroposophists and Theosophists, among others. That Dennis was a member of a Meditation Group which met there on a weekly basis is hardly surprising as it was a popular rendezvous, and a mixing bowl of esoteric ideas, both new and old. What is interesting if not surprising, is that the Meditation Group decided to leave the Quest Club for Etloe Road, which is not to say that Etloe Road was secondary, rather, it was just not obviously central to the life the Meditation Group knew and enjoyed.

The notice informs us that the Meditation Group had been running for a year or more at the Bristol Quest Club, and that the *Psycho-Physical healing Group* began at Etloe Road at some date after July 1948. We may be confident that it continued for some years after 1948, although where it was based is not clear. Indeed, the evidence suggests after 1954 it continued under the heading of the Order of St Raphael[3], and we may conclude, unless other information emerges to the contrary, that the *Psycho-Physical Healing Group* was the prototype of the Order of Dionysis & Paul.

---

3   Anson, Peter F. *Bishops at Large,* (London, Faber & Faber, 1964) p. 499

Assuming that 1948 constituted the beginnings of the proto-Order of Dionysis & Paul, then we have approximately seven years to account for before the earliest records available to us begin. (The Order of Dionysis & Paul Record Books begin in 1955.) From the few documents left in our care it is obvious that Dennis studied both personally and with a view to public life. In 1947 he had completed a course in *Medical Electricity* with the SMAE Institute of Medical Electricity. This, perhaps, reflects his work in the Psycho-spiritual healing group. Indeed, most of the studies he undertook in the early 1950's reflect the seriousness of this interest. In 1949 he completed a course of studies in *Metaphysics* with the Psychology Foundation of Great Britain. He completed two further courses in 1952: *Philosophy* with the Institute of Life Science, and *Psychology* with the Psychology Foundation of Great Britain. Dennis was a curious man with a broad range of interests, which this brief history will illustrate.

Mar Georgius

In the post-War years, Dennis was clearly moving away from the sphere of influence of the Hermes Temple. In due course he came into contact with Mar Georgius[4]; and although it is possible that he may have heard of him, or even met him during the War, the earliest records concerning any involvement date from the early 1950's. Mar Georgius was

Fig. 5. Mar Georgius   a significant influence upon Dennis. In 1953 Dennis was appointed as a Minister of the United Presbytery of the Fellowship of Christian Free Churches and began preaching in various churches around Bristol.

---

4   Hugh George de Willmott Newman, was born on 17 January 1905, in London, England. His family background was in the Catholic Apostolic Church (Irvingite). His father was a deacon in that church. Hugh George was baptised at the Catholic Apostolic Church at Mare Street, Hackney, London, England. He was educated at Crawford School, Camberwell, London, and later by private tuition. As a young man, he changed his name by deed poll to "de Willmott Newman", thus reflecting his mother's maiden name. Newman worked as a clerk in solicitors' offices until 1929.

Mar Georgius emerged quietly enough, being priested by Bishop James McFall of Belfast on the 23rd of October 1938. However, he later came to prominence, when on March 23, 1944, seeking to unite a group of British Churches, he established the *Western Orthodox Catholic Church*, the *Catholicate of the West*. On that day a Deed of Declaration united the *Ancient British Church*, the *Old Catholic Orthodox Church*, the *British Orthodox Catholic Church* and the *Independent Catholic Church* into a single organization known as *Catholicate of the West*.

This event would also have been important news for some of the circles that Dennis moved in. At the end of 1944, it was decided that the Catholicate would bring its ministry, organization, usages and worship into general conformity with the pattern and model of the Catholic Apostolic Church. The name *Catholic Apostolic Church (Catholicate of the West)* was adopted, with a subtitle "Western Orthodox Catholic Church", and the Catholic Apostolic Church's liturgy was adopted.

Inspired by Mar Georgius' vision, Dennis joined the *Catholicate of the West* in 1954, and was ordained by him in 1955. Their aspirations were full of the 'hope for change' that emerged with the end of that all-consuming War. It didn't last long though; their hopes were eroded over the course of time by the intransigence of the major Churches, who not only ignored them but also ridiculed them at every opportunity. To be fair to their critics it must be said that the antics of many of his clerics, provided most of the ammunition

Fig. 6. Mar Georgius.

for the criticism. Consequently, Mar Georgius' grand vision of a united Church, under the banner of the *Catholicate of the West* eventually dwindled away in 1968[5].

On the death of Mgr Williams, Archbishop of Caer-Glow, Mar Georgius asserted the claim that he was the legitimate successor of Archbishop Mathew, and therefore the head of the Old Roman Catholic Church in England. Alas, none of their branches were prepared to accept him as their ecclesiastical superior. This event disturbed Mar Georgius, and he withdrew from public life, arguably, to consider his position. Furthermore, the Catholicate seemed to be falling apart, thus, in 1953 he chose to dissolve the *Catholicate of the West*.[6] Later on, in 1959, the title, *Catholicate of the West*, was re-adopted by what was then called the United Orthodox Catholic Church. However, after a run of disruptive events the Catholicate was finally dissolved on the first of January 1968. Clearly, Mar Georgius had failed to control the ambitions of his senior clerics and suffered the consequences. Looking back, he felt able to write:

> "At its inception in 1944, it made one very big mistake,[7] in that it adopted the policy of attempting to unify *all* the so-called *episcopi vagantes*. Experience has proved this to be not only impossible, but undesirable, for oil and water cannot mix. Many bishops do not desire to be part of a disciplined Hierarchy, but prefer to adhere to the schismatic policy of so-called 'independence', a position utterly unknown to the Church of God. Others again do not accept the Catholic Faith, and the Catholicate has suffered much loss of reputation through being (though wrongly) identified in the public mind with the aberrations of such folk."[8]

The question is, were Mar Georgius and people like him naive hopefuls, or men 'before their time?' If we accept Anson's views, expressed in his book *Bishops at Large* then Mar Georgius and most of the clerics associated with him, would have been little

5   Anson, Peter F. *Bishops at Large*, (London, Faber & Faber, 1964) p. 491
6   *Ibid.*
7   i.e. The Catholicate
8   *Ibid.* p. 489-90

more than vain fools on a fool's errand, and so they might have been. Yet, despite having been ridiculed mercilessly by Anson's sardonic wit, arguably with the purpose of seeing them off, with their tails between their legs, curiously, and with the benefit of hindsight, they have had the audacity, not only to continue to exist fifty years later, but to have grown in numbers, whilst the major churches have markedly declined in numbers, credibility, and more importantly, in morality. I think the jury is still out on that question.

When we consider their behaviour we should bear in mind that it was not secular ambitions that inspired people such as Mar Georgius, they received little in the way of reward, of status or financial benefit. Misguided, perhaps, misinformed, definitely, over-reaching their abilities, clearly, and a few of them outright villains too! Yet, when all is said and done most of them were driven or inspired to do good for the sake of God and their fellows.

Not so long ago, we might have argued about whose side they were on, Satan's or God's, but today that question can be applied equally to all sides – Indeed, we may justifiably ask, who are the true followers of Christ today? With hindsight, it is easy to see how, in his unsympathetic and un-Christian-like book, Anson, reflected a common weakness of the Church hierarchy at large, which he unwittingly represents as being conceited, arrogant and dismissive of people's aspirations. Yet, when all is said and done, in spite of many failings and weaknesses, the numerous and erratic autocephalous churches do express something that is missing in the established churches. Belittle and deride them if you will, they yet continue to grow.

What is interesting is the sad fact that in the immediate aftermath of the War (1945), Mar Georgius had a wonderful opportunity to further his cause by assisting the many thousands of survivors of the War—both civilians and returning soldiers—if not with their physical injuries then with their emotional and spiritual problems, which were many. To engage in the 'cure of souls' at that time would have gone a long way to restoring people's faith in the Church. Instead, Mar Georgius directed his energies towards developing a hierarchy of what proved to be self-serving clerics, who had very little interest in serving their fellow man. Doubtless, he did not intend this to happen, but happen it did!

Like any other organisation, a Church is built around a person, or a team of people. Mar Georgius made the mistake of creating an organisation which looked impressive on paper, and tried to 'fit it out' with the 'right people'. Unfortunately, the right people all too frequently turned out to be the 'wrong people'. Clearly, he was not a good judge of character and was all too ready to take people at their word – a grave weakness as the history books show. In short he failed. He failed to achieve his primary life goal of uniting the Church and, more importantly, restoring the Catholic Apostolic Church, in which he grew up and to which he devoted his life to restore.

When I think about the life and work of Mar Georgius, I frequently reflect upon his obsession with ritual and the absolutely correct procedures involved – *style* rather than *content* – he seems to have been fixated by the outward form rather than the essential 'inner' meaning of a ritual. To be fair, it is a weakness that was not unique to him alone, it was, and is still, endemic among the Anglo-Catholic community; many of whom seek the esoteric facts and significance of ritual without acquiring sufficient understanding.

On the one hand, being more concerned with style and technique, I believe Mar Georgius stepped into this *cul-de-sac*, and became the miracle that never happened – the king that never was! On the other hand, his ambition to bring about the convergence of different historic lines of apostolic succession was fundamental to his quest for a unity of churches. In short, he had little choice. It may have been an ambition beyond his grasp or ability, but that clearly did not stop him trying. Why did he do it? I believe the short answer rests upon his conviction that he was divinely inspired, that he was moved by the Holy Spirit to achieve what many might think impossible. This is made clear in the following quotation. After the death of Dr Wilfred Maynard Davson, the last priest of the Catholic Apostolic Church, Mar Georgius wrote:

"The work of the LXX is now to commence, as foretold in prophetic utterances over all these years. But the work of preparation of those who are to participate therein demands one preliminary, and that is THEY MUST FIRST ACKNOWLEDGE THE RESTORED APOSTOLATE AS HAVING BEEN INDEED RAISED UP AND COMMISSIONED BY GOD. As one whose personal experience enables him to give a sure and certain testimony, I testify that the Work of the Restored XII was truly of God, though rejected of Christendom at large in their ignorance and sin" [9]

House Churches

It is a matter of fact that Mar Georgius could neither afford the grand buildings of the established Churches, nor were they readily available for him to let or to borrow. It was, then, to another more traditional approach that he naturally turned – that of House-churches. House churches are not a new phenomenon. Clearly, the Church at large began its communal life some 2000 years ago as a house-church, which simply means a room set aside in a dwelling for the faithful to engage in worship. The first house church is recorded in Acts 1:13, where the disciples of Jesus met together in the "Upper Room" (of a house). Several other passages in the New Testament specifically mention churches meeting in houses. For example, 1 Cor 16:19; Rom 16:3, 5; Col 4:15.

As the Church became established as an institution in medieval Europe, a house-church generally signified a private oratory in a dwelling belonging to a person of some means. In late medieval Europe, numbers of communities, such as The Brothers & Sisters of the Common Life,[10] were still centred around house-churches, rather than a local parish church. From the Reformation onwards, house-churches took a more significant path than before in that they also became the focal point of political awakening. Yet, in all cases a house-church has been a focal point of a spiritual community.

---

9   Mar Georgius, A Personal Statement Concerning His Mission, p.12. Glastonbury 1971. [Archives]
10   *Devotio Moderna, Basic Writings*, John Van Engen (trans.) Paulist Press, New York, 1988.

The origins of the modern house church movement in North America and the UK are varied. Some have described the movement as developing out of the Plymouth Brethren, whilst others identify the movement with Anabaptists, Quakers, Amish, Hutterites, Mennonites, Moravians and Methodists. Some think of the movement as a re-emergence of the Holy Spirit during the Jesus Movement of the 1970s in the USA or, the worldwide Charismatic Renewal of the late 1960s and 1970s. The truth is, to some degree they are all correct. Every newly-formed spiritual community is moved by the Holy Spirit, to join together for worship and for the dispensation of the sacraments in a space set aside – a sanctified space.

Returning to Anson for a moment, he was an erudite Roman Catholic who belonged to a traditional system of worship, wherein important people with appropriate titles, were to be found in large and frequently very ancient buildings. These buildings were sanctioned for worship by the Church and only the Church had the right to sanction them. Such are the traditions of the Church, and local/regional communities were expected to maintain such buildings as necessary. Mar Georgius was to all intents and purposes an interloper, like the others mentioned in Anson's book, and was treated harshly, which in Anson's view was absolutely the right thing to do from a corporate perspective, but not at all what Jesus might have done.

Today, many of these churches have been disposed of because they have proven to be just too large or expensive to maintain. The important, and generally more ancient churches, minsters, abbeys and cathedrals have been retained, but at a major and ongoing cost. However, fifty years and more later, a different situation has now emerged. With hindsight, we can see that from the end of the Second World War, as resources of time, money and labour have increased in cost, a movement towards smaller buildings and house-churches has spread out of necessity, and people such as Mar Georgius, consciously or unconsciously, were part of that movement. More and more people are turning their backs on the parish church institution, some of whom are gathering into smaller groups that in different ways are autonomous. It isn't simply the lack of funds that drives this movement, although that has often been a factor. A real sense of 'belonging' to a community is also important, A community in which the personal touch matters. Anson failed to recognise that emerging fact. This movement, driven both by economics and the need for a 'sense of community' is still of major importance.

Among the people referred to in Anson's book, few could afford large buildings, and many of necessity made do with smaller rooms or buildings. With regards to Mar Georgius, and to Dennis Green, Anson writes dismissively, for example:

"On January 6th, 1961, the administrative headquarters... were transferred to a modest dwelling-house at 12 Ashley Hill, Ashley Down, Bristol 6. One of its larger rooms was furnished as a pro-cathedral of the Supreme-Hierarchy... and his patriarchal throne translated from South Tottenham. The oratory was given the title of 'The Collegiate Church of the Epiphany and the Three Magi', and made a Chapel of Ease of the *Ecclesia Vetusta* at Glastonbury."[11]

and

"Although there were now eight dioceses in England and Wales, none of them, with the exception of Glastonbury, had so much as a pro-cathedral, and the Patriarch himself had to make do with a small domestic oratory at Kew, not having the hospitality of either St. Margaret's Roman Catholic Church in Pope's Grove or any of the nearby Anglican churches." [12]

It seems that in Anson's mind, he considered the endeavours of people such as Mar Georgius to be deluded or worse. What he did not comprehend was how, in the 1950's, a large number of 'Free Churches' would grow and flourish from such humble beginnings, how could he? Many of whom, from the outset, had decided that a church-building must be small, local, accessible and above all, affordable. After all, a Church is the 'people', not a

---

11   Anson, Peter F. *Bishops at Large*, (London, Faber & Faber, 1964) p. 499
12   *Ibid.* p..459

building. The terms: Cathedral, Pro-Cathedral, Abbey, Minster etc, are terms that describe the function of the apparatus not the majesty of an institution.

Dennis Green & The Emergence Of The Order

On April 10th Easter Sunday 1955, the Church of the Mystics was established at the Wesley Chapel, Wesley place, Durdham Downs, Bristol. The last service was held there on May 27th of that same year. In Dennis' own words:

> "The response had been sufficient to warrant a more permanent premises so arrangements have been made for the full use of the property owned by Mr Weaver, at No 4 Kellaway Avenue... Much work in decorating etc, ready for the opening on May 31st."[13]

Mar Georgius consecrated the church in July 1955. Gifts and contributions in support of this venture came from many sympathisers who were in various ways connected with Dennis and Esmé.[14] Although Esmé and Dennis were to separate at a later date, and Esmé was to later emigrate to Australia, at this stage, she seems to have been fully involved in this venture and committed resources and time to it.

At the request of Mar Georgius, the name of the Church was changed to: "*The Church of the Three Magi*". For three years the community of the Church of the Three Magi worked happily together at Kellaway Avenue. However, in August 1958, Mr Weaver gave Dennis notice and the Church of the Three Magi closed, the church furniture was put into storage, and the Church went into abeyance, but happily not for long. In October 1958, a large house was acquired by Dennis and Esmé at 12 Ashley Hill, Bristol. The furniture was withdrawn from storage and installed, and the church duly consecrated ready for the service on November the sixteenth, 1958. Dennis wrote an interesting comment in the Record Book (vol 1. p.2):

> "The same people were present who had assisted in the breakdown of the Church at Kellaway Avenue,

---

13   Records Vol. 1 p. 1
14   Records Vol. I. p. 1

so that the same collection of vibrations, which had taken so much time to establish at Kellaway Avenue, could be re-established at 12 Ashley Hill."

The Church was registered in Bristol (No. 67030) as the *Church of the Three Magi*. In January 1961 the name of the Church was changed from the Church of the Three Magi to *The Collegiate Church of the Epiphany and of the Three Magi*. Although Anson made a big thing of this in his book[15], it is merely noted in the Order Records.[16] The following year, on Tuesday 12th June 1962, the Order of St. Gilbert was installed at 12

Fig. 7. Rev Denis Green leaving Ashley Hill

Ashley Hill by Mar Georgius, with Dennis as its Prior. The Rev Peter Green, Colin Aitkins and Gerard Decieco, were also made brothers of the Order. This event required the Order to give up the name of the *Order of St Raphael*. One of the main features of this change of identity lay in the fact that it was a re-establishing of an English medieval monastic Order which had been open to both men and women, and as such was in keeping with one of the primary aims and objectives of the Order.

I have no way of ascertaining whether it came as a surprise to Dennis, as all of the people involved are dead, and the records are scanty, but No. 12 Ashley Hill, was put up for sale in July 1963,[17] presumably by Esmé. There is a letter in the archives dated 4th May 1964, written by Dennis to Esmé. It appears to be a

---

15   Anson, Peter F. *Bishops at Large*, (London, Faber & Faber, 1964), p. 499.
16   Records. Vol. 1. p. 11.
17   Records. Vol. 1. p. 15.

surprised response to the sale, but perhaps not, as it can also be read as an offer to acquire the house on the terms that they bought it. Whatever the letter's purpose, it clearly didn't work. They had been living separate lives for some time, Esmé in the upper house and Dennis on the ground floor, where the Chapel was located. One cannot help wondering just how much stress on their relationship had been caused by Mar Georgius and the Church, which I believe was the source of ill-will between Esmé and Dennis. Esmé did not like Mar Georgius, and he was probably the cause of much of the friction between them. Whether or not Dennis knew the house was to be sold is, in point of fact, irrelevant as he clearly found out over the course of time. What is relevant is that 'times were a'changing' and rapidly, as events were to demonstrate. In due course

Fig. 8. Desecrated chapel, Ashley Hill

the house was sold to Kenneth Thorn, a hypnotherapist – a singular event with serious repercussions.

On Jan 17th 1964, the Wessex Branch of the United Presbytery of Free Christian Churches was established at 12 Ashley Hill by Mar Georgius, with Dennis as the Moderator. The endeavour came to nothing and may well have been the tipping point between Dennis and Mar Georgius. It certainly appears to be the case that the nature and function of the Order of St Gilbert was taking upon itself a life of its own, a life in which Mar Georgius and the United Presbytery had no part to play. But first, a little more about Kenneth Thorn. Fate is a fickle thing, and just as matters were settling down, the new owner, Kenneth Thorn proved to be antagonistic to the aspirations of the Church doing all that he could to drive Dennis out of the building. At the end of 1964 Dennis entered the following in the Record Book:

Fig. 9. Rosary Priory

"We are experiencing great difficulty with the new owner of the house, Mr Kenneth Thorn, a hypnotherapist." [18]

It may not appear to be saying very much but on the 26th January 1965, Thorn had desecrated the chapel. The police were called and Thorn was 'cautioned' but with little effect. On Friday the 21st May, 1965, Thorn removed the baptismal font from the chapel, and in June further disturbances took place, with Thorn threatening Dennis with violence.

From the beginning of 1965, Dennis & Morris had been preoccupied with finding new premises, and in July of that year two cottages owned by British Railways were viewed and terms negotiated with estate agents at Wotton-Under-Edge, who acted on behalf of British Railways. A price of £200 was agreed for the two cottages and two acres of land situated at Pilning, Severn Beach, near Bristol. The price was low because there was a Closure-Order on the cottages. This did not deter the prospective buyers, and on acquiring the site from British Railways, everyone got 'stuck in' to make them fit for purpose. In due course the closure order was lifted, and on March 18th 1966, the Church

18   Records. Vol. 1, p. 17

moved to Pilning. On Saturday 2nd of April 1966, Dennis took up residence. Thereafter, the site was to be known as Rosary Priory.

Over the course of the following year a chapel was built for the use of the Order, by Br Ignatius. These were halcyon days when all seemed well with the world. However, Dennis' time with Mar Georgius had come to an end. His attempts to influence him over the years had come to nothing, which, in 1966, eventually led them to go their different ways. In 1967, subsequent to their parting company, Mar Georgius dissolved the Order of St Gilbert and released the brothers from his jurisdiction. Nevertheless, the Order continued to function as the Order of St Gilbert until 1982.

Whether he knew it or not, Mar Georgius had failed in his primary ambitions. Yet, in spite of his failure much was learned from his experience. The centralised and corporate structure of the Church at large was, and still is a major problem on all sorts of levels. From Mar Georgius' perspective emulating the established Churches was an error – he was emulating a model that was already in decline. Indeed, after 1945 history was unfolding a different pattern in which 'small is beautiful'; the future lay in paying attention to its unfolding structure. The truth is that 'small' survives because it can be supported effectively and in the long-term by a small number of people. By not recognising this, Mar Georgius missed an opportunity. 'Small is beautiful' also works because it is both personal and manageable, and in such an environment people feel a genuine part of a religious community. Interconnected autonomous groups, following a creed they love and understand, is far more desirable than a corporate culture, which demands the faithful to conform to a rigid and difficult to understand theology.

On parting company from Mar Georgius, Dennis joined the Western Orthodox Church under the authority of Mar Phillipus (Bishop Singer), and was consecrated to the Episcopate by him in June 1967 as Mar Dionysis of Aust. Sadly, in 1968 he was diagnosed as having cancer of the throat, and he was admitted into hospital for surgery. I am reasonably convinced that Dennis went into hospital with every intention of returning to active life after his operation. However, as events transpired, he did not. Extensive surgery during the latter part of 1968 did nothing to halt the cancer, and his condition continued to deteriorate, until his death at ten minutes past twelve on 4th September 1970.

No organisation is ever totally free of negative influences. This is especially true at its beginning and at critical moments in its development. One such influence was Frank Cowell, an Australian by birth, whom I first met in the mid-1970s, by which time he had retired from his career as a draughtsman. Frank was a high Anglican by inclination (he attended a very ritualistic church: St. Mary's in Tyndall's Park), a theologian by nature, and a very well read and enthusiastic man – with a vast and chaotic theological library.

Precisely when Frank arrived 'on the scene' is unclear, but by the mid-sixties he was noted as being an argumentative and cantankerous individual who would split theological hairs to pass the time, and he knew all too well how to bear a grudge! This was not so much of a problem in general terms, but it was a problem at Order meetings, where people gathered to explore the spiritual dimensions of their lives and were rarely concerned with the finer points of theology or, indeed, of history.

The records show (Vol. 1. p.17 & 19) that he was formally asked to stay away from such meetings because of his disruptive behaviour. Yet Frank must have been fond of the Order for he maintained contact, generally on friendly terms, until he joined the Russian Orthodox Church in Bristol at some time in the 1980's. Frank Cowell[19] was a strange man, quick to argue and take offence, but for all that, he was a kind and thoughtful person who went out of his way to help the Order. During the horrendous conflict of interests that took place at number 12 Ashley Hill, between Thorne and Dennis, Frank was instrumental in finding

---

19   **Frank Cowell** appears in different guises and with different names throughout the history of the Order – forever the same, passionately arguing and splitting hairs about issues no-one else is really interested in. If such people were empathic and able to control their behaviour, they would be a valuable asset, yet they never do; they are invariably 'driven out', one way or another, by the members who attend for clearly different reasons. Members such as Brothers John and Lazarus, who could have been the grit that stimulates the oyster to produce a 'pearl of great price', over-played their concerns and discovered how little their 'opinions' meant to the members at large.

the cottages at Pilning that became Rosary Priory. He was also responsible for building a temporary chapel using materials from Ashley Hill.

A Change of Administration

Dennis died without consecrating anyone to succeed him as Bishop, but he did appoint Fr Gerard Decieco (Br Ignatius), to succeed him as the Abbot of the Order. This meant that the Order, then the Order of St Gilbert, was without religious jurisdiction and without episcopal oversight. Furthermore, Br Ignatius did not endear himself to the other members. So much so that many of them withdrew and he was left on his

Fig. 10. Fr Gerard Decieco

own at Rosary Priory – especially after he contested the Will. As I understand it, Br Ignatius contested Dennis' Will, which Dennis had signed unwitnessed, and in which he had left Rosary Priory and all other effects to the members of the Order. When and how he actually challenged the Will I do not know; however, solicitors being what they are, such things take a considerable time to process. Thus, the records show that on the 26ᵗʰ February 1974, the Will was declared invalid.[20] The estate then reverted to Dennis' wife, Esmé, who passed the estate on to Br Ignatius for and on behalf of the Order.

Br Ignatius contesting the Will has always been something of a mystery. He had served Dennis and the Order faithfully for many years, yet his actions in challenging the Will, seem to contradict everything he stood for. Nevertheless, challenge it he did and it will always remain a mystery, unless, of course we consider the following. In 1970, following Dennis' death, the Order surrendered any claim to ownership of the Priory to Br Ignatius. Perhaps this fact lay at the heart of the matter – he felt obligated to do so! As mentioned earlier, Fate is a fickle old thing. In the early 1980's Rosary Priory was compulsorily purchased by

20   Records. Vol. 2, p. 6

the local council and became the site for the English side of the second Bridge into Wales. The last I saw of it, the derelict Rosary Priory sat directly under the ascending ramp of that bridge. It was left to Fr Morris Saville to continue the development of the Order.

Throughout 1969-70 it became increasingly clear that Dennis was going to die. At the time, the numbers of members had been relatively consistent – approximately a dozen or so – however, as the year 1970 progressed, and as the members realised that they would be relying upon Br Ignatius for spiritual guidance, their faith wavered and some of them resigned. Fortunately, standing quietly in the background was Fr Morris Saville, and as it proved, it was upon his shoulders that the mantle of the Spirit fell to carry the Order forward through some very interesting times.

Father Morris Saville

Fig. 11. Fr Morris Saville

I first met Fr Morris Saville in the autumn of 1975 at an Order discussion group that met regularly, twice a week, at his home in Armada House, Cotham, Bristol. I had been introduced to this group by Stephen Gunstone, then an active member of the Order. What struck me most about Fr Morris was his 'spiritual presence', which was strong, steady, quiet and informed (so it seemed to me). I had spent years wandering from group to group, from movement to movement, looking for 'something' that could validate the 'spiritual life'. Until I met Fr Morris, I had encountered little more than a motley collection of self-serving people looking for an audience and an easy life, so meeting him was both a relief and a blessing. Fr Morris was a different kind of man all together, he proved to be a quiet and thoughtful person who considered the effect of his actions or words before he acted or spoke. He was also a methodical thinker and planner who recognised the restrictions of a given economy. But, above all his love of the

Spirit, and of the spiritual life was without bounds. I knew without doubt I had found what I was looking for. Over a few weeks my conviction grew, and when I broached the subject of studying with him, he suggested I take three months to consider whether I was sure I wanted to follow this path.

On April 17th, 1976, I was initiated, and if my memory serves me right, the membership at that time consisted of: Br Francis (prior); Sr Claudia; Br Ignatius (prior); Br Michael; Br Barnabas; Br Joseph; Sr Frances; Br William; Br Wilfred, and myself, Br Marcus. There may have been a few others, but their names have faded; Moreover, several on this list were then inactive or in abeyance, and, as time passed some of them resigned.

Br Francis, (the Order name of Fr Morris) had an amazing grasp of all things spiritual, and his ability to convey that spiritual sense was equally profound. As is often the case, those with real spiritual understanding often carry some form of burden, and Br Francis was no exception. He suffered from a dreadful inherited affliction, *Hereditary Hemorrhagic Telangiectasia,* also known as

Fig. 12. Br Francis

the Osler–Weber–Rendu disease. It is a rare autosomal dominant genetic disorder that leads to abnormal blood vessel formation in the skin, mucous membranes, and often in organs such as the lungs, liver, and stomach. This meant that he bled, usually internally, and apart from blood-transfusions there was little that the medics could do to stop it. They even tried laser surgery to cauterise the bleeding, but to no avail. In due course the disease grew progressively worse until it finally killed him.

Throughout the time I knew him Br Francis worked in the secular world as a clerk for National Westminster Bank in their Stocks and Shares Deptament. In his own words, "it provides enough for my needs, without too much demand". Which was fortunate as his health was in decline; *Hereditary Hemorrhagic Telangiectasia* is a condition that becomes significantly worse as time passes – the older you get the worse it becomes. Fortunately, before his health forced him to retire, he purchased a house in South Bristol, which served as a home for himself, his wife Christine, and for the Order.

However, I am getting ahead of myself. On the death of Dennis, Br Francis found himself having to deal with several problems. The first was religious jurisdiction, to what religious body did the Order belong? The second was a lack of episcopal oversight, because Dennis had died without consecrating anyone to oversee the Order or to continue the line. Third, who was the head of the Order? Dennis had appointed Br Ignatius as Abbot, but no-one would follow him, and last but not least, the Order no longer had a home because Br Ignatius had taken Rosary Priory as his own.[21] I later discovered that some of the members that I encountered in 1975/6 were frustrated by this situation and had left because of Br Ignatius.

Rebirth

Dennis had died in 1970 and Br Francis spent the first years of his administration looking for religious jurisdiction. I understand now what a frustrating and time-consuming journey 'around the houses' it must have been to achieve this, but it was done, and not before time. So, when I was initiated in 1976, I was initiated into the Order of Saint Gilbert, which had been accepted the previous year into the Reformed Catholic Church, under Arch-Bishop Donald Garner. Thus, Br Francis had achieved religious jurisdiction within the Reformed Catholic Church, and episcopal oversight under Garner's authority.

The question of authority 'within' the Order was more complicated. Dennis had appointed the Rev Gerard Decieco (Br Ignatius) to succeed him as the Abbot of the Order, however, the records show that on 23rd of April 1973, Br Ignatius relinquished that office in favour of Prior. On the 7th of December, 1976, he resigned his position in both the Church and the Order, and again on 13th December 1982.[22] It seemed to me that never was a man less suited for the office of an Abbot or Prior. During those years the issue of authority niggled at almost everything that took place within the Order and Br Ignatius was usually at the

---

21   Records, 2, p. 32, 33,
22   Records, Vol, 2. p. 3, 21,

centre of it. For instance, without consulting the other members of the Order, Br Ignatius formally applied to the Liberal Catholic Church for membership.

Initially his application was refused on the basis that the Liberal Catholic Church had no opening for an Order. He then approached Bp Burton and asked for his assistance. This approach seems to have been successful because from Friday 23rd July 1971 the Order became an Affiliated Community of the Liberal Catholic Church. On Sunday the 25th of July 1971, they celebrated Mass (Liberal Catholic Church liturgy, I assume) with the attendance of Br Francis and Fr Peter Carvel, who represented Bp James Burton and the Liberal Catholic Church.

Br Ignatius states[23] that he had asked Br Francis and the other members to assist him prepare for the official opening on Sunday the twenty-fifth, making the point that not one member attended or helped. Indeed, the only person who assisted him was ninety-year-old Dora Hart. The question, it is fair to ask, is Why? The answer is given, in part, on page 11 of volume two of the records, and points to the erratic behaviour of Br Ignatius being at the root of the problem. It is dated Wednesday the 15th of January 1975. It records that a synod was held to discuss Br Ignatius' letter to bishop James Burton, requesting that he should become a Liberal Catholic priest and abandon the Order of St Gilbert, etc. Shortly after that synod, Order members were informed by Bp Burton, that Br Ignatius had untruthfully written to him stating the Order of St Gilbert had disbanded some eighteen months previously. As a result of Br Ignatius' erratic behaviour, a letter was sent by Br Francis (Feb. 2 1975) dissolving the Affiliation. Bp Burton replied with the sentiment 'he thought it wise'.[24] The Affiliation with the Liberal Catholic Church had lasted three and a half years (1st July 1971 – 2nd Feb. 1975)[25]

However, politics apart, one of the great joys of a religious community is when a new member is initiated into their midst, and Stephen Gunstone was no exception. He was initiated

---

23   Records, Vol, I. p. 27, 28.
24   Records, Vol. 2, p. 11
25   Records, Vol. 2, p. 12

into the Order on Tuesday the 9th of May, 1972. Stephen was a gifted 'sensitive' although his gift proved to be a curse too. Like many sensitives, he had a lot of trouble focussing upon the curriculum and maintaining the 'discipline' of the Order.

On Saturday the 28th of May 1972, Christine Chapman was also initiated. As fate would have it, Br Francis and Christine were eventually married on Monday the 27th of April, 1974, at Quakers Friars Registry Office, Bristol. A Church Wedding at Rosary Priory followed on Sunday 8th of September, 1974. It was a happy marriage that sadly ended when Br Francis died in 1991.

Life was clearly moving on for the Order. Br Francis had lived something of a quiet monastic life at 96 Cotham Brow, Bristol, wherein he had quite naturally established an oratory, but on Monday the 21st of November, 1972, it was closed down, pending his removal to 58 Armada House, Kingsdown, where a new life was to emerge. On the 23rd of November a new oratory was consecrated, dedicated to the Alpha et Omega & His Holy Angels.

On Saturday the 21st of April 1973, Michael Startup was initiated at Rosary priory. Michael was an interesting man. He too was a 'sensitive', and he was thoughtful, as well being a keen writer. I believe he was studying psychology at Bristol University and was an enthusiastic observer of human behaviour, however, his sensitivity, instead of strengthening him, disturbed him and he eventually left the Order to follow a secular path.

Br Ignatius had succeeded Dennis as the Abbot. A title he relinquished in favour of Prior, on Monday the 23rd of April 1973. This was the first of many such irrational actions over the years. This particular act became interesting rather than typical when it transpired that he had challenged the validity of Dennis Green's Last Will and Testament. It is reported in the Records (Vol. II, p.6) that on the 26th of February, 1974, the Will had been declared invalid by Br Ignatius' solicitor. The Rosary Priory estate then became the property of Esmé Green, Dennis' widow, who declared it would be transferred to the Order as Dennis wished. However, on the 18th of August 1975, she felt it necessary to write a letter to Br Ignatius (with a copy sent to Br

Francis), reminding him that he should allow other members to use the Priory, *as is their right!* (V2, p. 14)

These were relatively busy times for Br Francis as the following activities described in the Records illustrate. They are provided to convey a sense of what was taking place. Many have been omitted as they are simply domestic, and don't bear repeating, whilst others are repetitive, and shall be avoided to avoid unnecessary tedium.

On Friday the 28th of June 1974, Janet Tyler, Mary Frances McDonald and Lesley Gunstone were initiated into the Order. Stephen Gunstone was also reinstated after a period of twenty-one months release from the Order. More good news followed when on the 17th of April 1975 the Order was accepted into the Reformed Catholic Church. This was followed on the 18th of May, when representatives of the Order and the Reformed Catholic Church met at the latter's Swindon Mission. The leader of the mission, the Very Rev Len Smith, formally accepted the clergy of the Order of St Gilbert into the Reformed Catholic Church. Br Ignatius was appointed to oversee missions in the South West, and Br Francis to administer to the Order of St Gilbert.[26]

Gerald Wills was received into the Church and into the Order on the first of August, 1975. On the 2nd of September, William Seeney was also received back into the Order, having been in abeyance. On Easter Saturday, (17th of April 1976) during the celebration of Mass, Allan Armstrong was initiated into the Order, and on Saturday the 5th of June 1976, Patricia Moffatt was received into the Church, and Deirdre Green was baptised.

I must assume that the Very Reverend Len Smith of the Reformed Catholic Church, died between the nineteenth of May and the beginning of November 1975, because on the 18th of November of that year Br Francis was appointed Vicar General to fill the vacancy left by the *late* Very Rev Len Smith. On the 6th of August 1976, during the celebration of Holy Mass, the Order of St Gilbert was declared defunct and all membership terminated, and the *Apostolic Order of the Three Magi*, was

---

26   Records, Vol. 2, p. 18.

inaugurated by Br Francis. On the 7th of September 1976, Janet Tyler and Mary McDonald resigned their membership to join the Celtic Church under Bishop Singer. The two events were not directly connected.

On the 7th of December 1976, Br Ignatius resigned from both the Reformed Catholic Church, and from the Order. Why? He had been accepted by Fr Peter Morgan to study for three years and to receive re-training and re-ordination as a Roman Catholic priest, for the dissident Tridentine Movement. He was expected to sell the Priory to that organisation to be used as a Tridentine Mass Centre. However, in February 1977, for reasons we can now only guess at, Fr Peter Morgan wrote to Br Ignatius refusing him entry into the Roman Catholic Tridentine movement. He was then without membership of any church.

Alan Bain was received into the Reformed Catholic Church during Mass at the Alpha et Omega on Friday, 17th of December 1976. On the 28th of January 1977, he received the orders of Tonsured Clerk and Doorkeeper, his first steps towards becoming a priest of the Reformed Catholic Church, wherein he hoped to be provided with the authority to create a new order and community. Abp Donald Garner had agreed to this in principle.

On the 3rd of September 1977, at the Mission of St James, London, both Alan Bain and Allan Armstrong were raised to the order of deacon. On Saturday 24th December, the new chapel at 31 Hill Avenue was dedicated to Alpha et Omega, and during the celebration of Holy Mass Br Ignatius was also received back into the Reformed Catholic Church as an archpriest, on the decision of Abp Donald Garner. On Good Friday,  the 24th of March 1978 the temple of the Alpha et Omega, at 31 Hill Avenue, was consecrated. On Saturday the 8th of July 1978, Allan Armstrong was ordained to the priesthood by Abp Donald Garner at the Mission of St James, London.

Fig. 13. Abp Donald Garner

Just as things were progressing smoothly, and all was well with the world, Br Francis received a letter on Friday the 20th of October 1978, from Abp Donald Garner, accusing him of 'teaching Heresy'. The letter also stated, in Donald's own words, "I think we should split – it is the only way."[27] A meeting was called to discuss this situation and the consensus was that the Order should separate from the Reformed Catholic Church. Thus, on Sunday, the 22nd of October 1978, a letter was sent by Br Francis accepting Donald's wishes. A copy of this letter is in the archives.

One of the great highlights of 1979 took place on Saturday the 27th of January. A Wedding Mass was celebrated at the Alpha et Omega, for Allan & Gloria Armstrong, who had previously married in the Registry office in 1970. They renewed their vows in the context of the Blessed Sacrament of Marriage according to the Catholic Rite. It was a quiet and joyful occasion.

However, not so pleasant news was to follow; Hugh George de Willmott-Newman, (Mar Georgius) Patriarch Metropolitan of Glastonbury, of the Orthodox Church of the British Isles, died on Wednesday the 28th of February, 1979. He was Moderator of the United Presbytery of Christian Free Churches and Sovereign Grand Master of the Teutonic Order of the Levant; He was also initiated into the mysteries of the Western Tradition, and held important positions in Freemasonry. The Glastonbury Rite, compiled by him, has remained the official Mass of our community.

After some correspondence with Abp. Garner, the Order was received back into the Reformed Catholic Church on the 19th of August 1980. On the following Sunday (the 24th), the Order of the Three Magi was dissolved during the celebration of Holy Mass, in favour of the *Reformed Catholic Church Society*. Then, alas, on Saturday 14th of February, 1981 Abp. Donald William Garner died in University College Hospital, London.

The records show[28] that a special Synod was held on Sunday the 29th of March at South Hill Park, Hampstead, London, where it was agreed by all of the members of the Synod, that the

27   Records, Vol. 2. p. 33
28   Records, Vol. 2. p. 46

Reformed Catholic Church Society was deemed to have ceased to exist upon the death of the late Primus Donald Garner. It was also made known to us that the arrangements made with him with regards to the Order had not been passed on to the Synod. In view of which we announced we would be known as the Order of Dionysis & Paul the Apostle.

The conflict continued and the undercurrents were becoming unbearable. It was clear that the Reformed Catholic Church was uncertain about what to do with the Order. After some discussion among the members of the Order it was decided that it was better in the long-run to resign from the Reformed Catholic Church, and on the 28th of August 1982, Br Francis wrote to Bp Ian Kirk-Stewart tendering our resignation. (What re-inforced this act was the recognition that the ongoing conflict with the Reformed Catholic Church was taking its toll on Br Francis, his health was deteriorating so much that in August 1982, Order meetings were suspended because of this).

Concurrent with the above, Sr Frances recommended that we should write to Bp Williams asking to be incardinated into the Holy Celtic Church.[29] However, before that could happen a Protocol of Election, and Mandate for the Consecration of Br Francis, was sent on Saturday 22nd of May, 1982, to Bp Anthony Clements of the Holy Celtic church. The intention was that the Order of St Gilbert would become incardinated into the Holy Celtic Church with its own bishop-abbot.[30]

Fig. 14. Sr Frances

Coincidentally, on the 19th of November 1982, the use of the name 'Order of St Gilbert' was challenged by Seraphim, the successor to Mar Georgius. The Order met and decided that the message was clear – the Lord did not want us involved with the Reformed Catholic Church or with the name of the Order of St Gilbert, and although Seraphim had little grounds to make his

---

29   Records, Vol. 2. p. 50
30   Records, Vol. 2, p. 52

claim, the members agreed to change the name to the Order of Dionysis & Paul – a name suggested some years earlier by the late Dennis Green[31].

Once again Br Ignatius was up to his silly tricks. On Sunday the 5th of December 1982, he initiated Colin Richens into the Order, which on the face of it was a good thing. Unfortunately, the initiation was invalid because no members were present as witnesses and Br Ignatius did not use an official liturgy. Br Ignatius clearly didn't like the Order's response and he replied by sending an aggressive letter to Sr Claudia justifying the events of the previous Sunday. Consequently, on Monday the 13th of December 1982, Br Ignatius and his ministers were released from both the Holy Celtic Church and the Order.

On the 17th of December 1982, Br Francis was admitted to Ward 24 of the Bristol Royal Infirmary with heart problems. He was released to come home on Christmas Eve. He subsequently had several such attacks over the next few years. Fortunately, he did not require surgery as the problem was resolved with drugs.

On Sunday the 5th of September, 1982, after a considerable period of time making arrangements in good faith, Br Francis was fraudulently raised to the episcopacy at the Liberal Catholic Church of St Raphael, Birmingham, by Raymond Anthony Clements. It took a little while for the truth to emerge, that Clements was not in fact a bishop, but emerge it did. A letter was received on the second of August 1983, from Archbishop Vicktor Ivan Busa, of Palermo. The letter stated that Clements was a *Bishop Elect*, but not consecrated. This letter proved that Clements was not consecrated a bishop by Abp Busa.[32] Following an Episcopal Synod, called by bishop R Swingler, of the Liberal Catholic Church, Clements resigned from that Church for fraudulently providing Br Francis with the episcopacy for the Holy Celtic Church. This was indeed a sad day for our community, but one good thing to have happened was that we had inherited, by agreement with Bishop Anthony

31   Records, Vol. 2, p. 55
32   Records, Vol. 2. p. 69.

Williams, the Holy Celtic Church, for which rite we had to seek episcopal oversight.

Fig. 15. Sr Claudia

Sr Frances telephoned Bishop Morrell of Nottingham on Saturday the 13th of August 1983, who said he was agreeable to re-consecrate Br Francis to the episcopacy and re-ordain Eric Eades. It was confirmed by telephone with Bp Morrell that the date of the consecration would be in Bristol, on Saturday the 3rd of September, 1983.[33] However, Morrell withdrew his promise, and on Sunday the 28th of September, Sr Claudia wrote to Bishop Hurgon of the Reformed Catholic Church; he too made his excuses.

On Tuesday the 20th of September, 1983, a telephone call was made to Abp Illtyd Thomas of the Celtic Catholic Church requesting help to regularise the situation. On Friday the 30th of September, Abp Illtyd Thomas visited Bristol. After a long discussion about the current dreadful state of affairs, Illtyd offered to consecrate Br Francis as Archbishop for the Holy Celtic Church. Thus, on Sunday the 9th of October 1983, in the chapel of the Alpha et Omega in Bristol, Br Francis was consecrated as Mar Francis, Bishop of the Holy Celtic Church by Archbishop Illtyd Thomas. Our small community now had valid episcopal oversight and was at last free of bishops who would play pointless headgames with us.

In spite of the good fortune that was bestowed upon the Order by Abp Illtyd Thomas, Mar Francis' health continued to decline and he was to spend more and more time in hospital, receiving blood-transfusions and other essential medical assistance. Over the next decade he had more than a dozen heart-related issues and other debilitating episodes. Nevertheless, Order life continued with his support, and with a growing community of brethren. When he was unable to lead a meeting, then Br Marcus would run meetings at his home in Kingsdown, Bristol; something that happened more and more as time passed.

33   Records, Vol 2, p. 70, 71

Life continued apace, with Mar Francis and Sr Claudia arranging for Eric Eades to be ordained on Saturday the 3rd of December 1983, by Illtyd Thomas, assisted by Br Marcus and Ian Kacyoroski. On Wednesday the 6th of June 1984, Br John was baptised in preparation for his initiation into the Order, which took place at the Alpha et Omega on Wednesday the 24th of October 1984.

On Saturday the 22nd of September, 1984, The Holy Celtic Church held its annual Synod at Hill Avenue. The most contentious issue on the agenda being the subject of women priests. The majority voted against, including Mar Francis. Change comes slowly! On Wednesday the 19th of June 1985, the Glastonbury Mass 1984, had its first 'airing' at the chapel of the Alpha et Omega. Br Marcus celebrated. All who attended thought it a success and it has been in use ever since.

Whilst the members of the Order generally maintained their spiritual discipline of engaging in the Offices, of study and coming together for meetings and communal worship, Sr Claudia, because of her artistic talents, was able to interpret aspects of Order life in a unique fashion. Apart from various portraits of order members, and her meditative interpretations of various spiritual themes rendered into a visual form, Sr Claudia also became the focal point and source of what is now called the *FDP Herald*. The idea of producing a monthly magazine had been in circulation for some time, bubbling under the surface, as it were, but with one thing and another it never really emerged, until 1985, when Sr Claudia's design for the cover of *The Celtic Tablet* was completed and distributed to members in September, 1985. This advance production was to encourage members to produce articles for inclusion.

Fig. 16. The Celtic Tablet.

The first issue of *The Celtic Tablet* came out on Wednesday the 20th of November, 1985. Since

Fig. 17. Sr Martha

then, it has had many forms. It was edited firstly by Sr Claudia, then Br Marcus, followed by Br Francis, and then by Br Johanan. Its latest form being an online magazine, under the banner of the *FDP Herald*, edited by Br James. It is hosted on our website, *www.ecclesiasticaceltica.org.* As ever, with any such enterprise, finding regular contributors of articles and stories is tricky, to say the least, especially from contemplatives such as members of the Order.

On Sunday the 22nd of December, Mar Francis, assisted by Sr Frances and Sr Claudia, consecrated the "The Chapel of Ease to Our Lord and St Francis" at Dudden House, Bristol Road, Paulton, Avon. In 1986 two baptisms took place at the Alpha et Omega. On Tuesday the 15th of April that of Br Solomon was administered by Br Marcus and celebrated by Mar Francis, while Br Matthias was baptised, also by Br Marcus, on Tuesday the 4th of November.

By this time the ordination of women had been accepted, and on Wednesday, 31st July 1986, Sr Martha (Pat Moffat) was ordained by Mar Francis. Subsequent to her ordination, Sr Martha moved to Fort William, Scotland, and began to build a Church community there, an enterprise that ended prematurely when she died of cancer on 13th January 1991. On Pentecost, Sunday 7th June 1987, Sr Claudia was ordained to the priesthood, with Mar Francis as celebrant, and during this Mass Br Matthias was initiated into the ODP. On the 22nd May, 1988, Mar Francis and Abp Illtyd Thomas consecrated Allan Armstrong as a Bishop for the Holy Celtic Church.

On the 10th of May 1991, after a long period of ill-health, Abp Morris Saville died peacefully at home, leaving his 'Watch in good order.'

Of him it is written:

"Within him was found the rare quality of supremely great mystical illumination and great intellectual power, which he used to share his wisdom with any who approached him with

an open heart, and like a midwife he conscientiously nurtured those seeds, planted in the minds of the brotherhood, helping them to give birth to their true spiritual selves." [34]

On Wednesday the 26th of June, 1991, his ashes were scattered at sea, in the Bristol Channel, from a workboat called 'Pill Cobbler Run'.

"Three members of the Order of Dionysis & Paul, the Rt Reverend Br Marcus, the Reverend Br Matthias and the Reverend Sr Claudia, hired a workboat to take them out into the Bristol Channel as far as Walton Signal Station, to scatter Mar Francis' Ashes.

We journeyed out upon 'choppy waters'. It had been raining for several days; dark clouds were above but no rain was falling. When we arrived just past Walton Signal Station, the engines were cut off to enable us to perform the ceremony.

As we began, a stillness was felt, a presence which brought joy, the sun shone brilliantly, unexpectedly, through the dark clouds reflecting off the water. The Spirit was with us as the ashes were scattered ceremoniously. We closed with prayers and the boatman headed back to Portbury Dock."[35]

Fig. 18. Sr Claudia and Br Matthias returning from scattering the Ashes of Mar Francis. (Br Marcus taking photo)

34   Records, 2. p. 114
35   *Ibid.*

The Order of Dionysis & Paul

On Saturday the 21st of September 1991, Bp Marcus was installed as the new Archbishop of the Holy Celtic Church.

Before describing the Order of Dionysis & Paul in any detail, it is important to look at its emergence over the course of the last 70 years. The Order had clearly emerged into the world against great odds, and it may seem strange that it emerged as it did, a fusion of two spiritual forces that in many respects appear to have failed, but arguably, it is only out of these two spheres that it could have emerged.

The spiritual forces I refer to are the exoteric and esoteric aspects of religion. The exoteric need no introduction except to say it is well-known to in the form of the world's leading Christian churches, such as the Roman Catholic Church and the Church of England, that have changed so much to their apparent detriment over the years. The esoteric aspects have many fantastic forms, but when all is said and done they derive either from the monastic elements of the Church, which have been in decline for decades, or the Rosicrucian and Hermetic streams of thought that populate the shadow-lands of our society. What they have to offer, where useful, is mostly of a secondary nature.

That the Order emerged is one thing, which has already been explained in part and requires little further explanation, but why it emerged is another, and that does require explanation. It could be said quite fairly that the Church in its decline is suffering the consequences of its errors. The most significant being a loss of direction, by which I mean that the purpose of religion is not simply the worship of God through the agency of an elite priesthood, but to assist the growth and development of the soul through Prayer, Meditation and the development of a spiritual *habitus*, which is, after all, how the Church began.

When the Church first emerged it had few resources, yet it had sufficient strength to expand in spite of the might of the Roman Empire, and more importantly, against a universal pagan mind-set. That it did so is a matter of history. Indeed the centuries before Constantine witnessed a progressive development of a strong, patient and robust Church that was in no hurry to go anywhere or to do anything except practise a virtuous life. Yet, over the course of the centuries the Church seems to have lost both its strength and its sense of purpose, which is perhaps understandable, but what is difficult to comprehend is that it refuses to engage with its errors, focussing instead upon the demands of popular culture—*form without substance*—something that would never have happened in the primitive Church — to which I draw your attention to the Gnostic conflict, past and present, as an example.

Change is inevitable, but it was only after the second World War that the desire for change quickened sufficiently to overcome the gravitational mass of social inertia. The Order has a particular form that emerged and has survived. The reason why constitutes the very basis of tradition—*maintaining connectivity with its roots, not just with its essence, but also with its form and energies*—on these terms the word 'evolution' itself presupposes tradition.

The Order established and maintained its connection with the Church and its rituals because in its '*essence*' the Church is strong, even when its energies are misdirected, and its form weak. It is a fair criticism that as the Church evolved over the centuries it lost touch with its essence by paying too much attention to the outward forms of worship in which its energies are dissipated, and thereby weakened – in short it has focussed upon the outward show of worship, but omitted to cultivate Prayer, Meditation and a Spiritual *Habitus* in the souls of the faithful. Thus, in describing the Order of Dionysis & Paul, it must be emphasised that its primary purpose has ever been to promote the growth and development of the soul through Prayer, Meditation and the cultivation of a Spiritual *Habitus*. Everything else is secondary.

Its essence is the same as it was two thousand years ago, although its energies and form vary according to the needs of time and place. Such 'Work' (cultivating a new *Habitus*) does not require a great number of members, but they must be true to it, for only by being true to the Work does that critical 'spiritual ferment' take place. Membership is more than being initiated into the Order. It is in many ways a state of being. In times past, some of the members joined, left and rejoined, others have stayed the course and one or two have joined and have never been seen again; but none of those who were initiated have been left unchanged.

What was, and is still expected of a member, is to engage in the daily offices, to study the curriculum and to attend Order meetings both for discussion and for worship. It has ever been understood that in following this approach members will begin to develop a behavioural reflex that is not defined by the instinctive nature of the first Adam, but is determined by the spiritual nature of the second Adam. What this means is to develop a nature that rests upon the principle of empathy and compassion rather than the selfish aspirations of the instinctive nature. This is no easy task, nor is it something that happens quickly. Our behavioural reflex – our *habitus* is built into the very fibres of our being and it takes a considerable time to sublimate a reflex that we have cultivated over many years.

The word *habitus* is a Latin translation of the Greek word *hexis*, used by Aristotle to mean the acquired virtues of temperance, fortitude, justice and prudence, which are the prerequisites for a virtuous life. The term was re-introduced to modern usage by the anthropologist Marcel Mauss (1872-1950) to mean those aspects of culture that are anchored in the daily practices of individuals and groups, including the learned habits, bodily skills, styles, tastes, and other non-discursive knowledge for a specific group. *Habitus* represents the way group culture and personal history shape the body and the mind, and as a consequence, shape society. In the 1960s the French sociologist Pierre Bourdieu adapted the word *Habitus* to describe human relations and why we are like we are. He thought that for most people, their *habitus* was to all intents and purposes permanent. However the best contemporary definition outside of secular culture, is by the late Alan Kreider, who discusses it at length in his book *The Patient Ferment*.[36]

---

36   *The Patient Ferment of the Early Church,* Alan Kreider, Baker Academic, Grand Rapids, Michigan, 2016.

The life of the Order is an expression of the Rule, the first part of which states: *Seek first the Kingdom of God*[37]. It is to this singular purpose that the Order is dedicated. What it actually means is that we should adapt our way of life, our *habitus*, by following the teachings of the Lord Jesus Christ, who taught that the *Kingdom of God is within you.*[38] In short, the Lord taught that by meditating or reflecting upon our traditional manner of behaviour and by comparing it with the standards and examples He set, we are able to modify our reactive patterns of behaviour, and thereby evolve into a more integrated human being. The second part of the rule states:

> *"Thou shalt love the Lord thy God with all of thy heart*
> *and with all of thy soul and with all of thy mind and*
> *with all of thy strength, and that Thou shalt love thy*
> *neighbour as thy self"*[39]

In this statement is outlined the *habitus* of the second Adam: to love God is not simply to think kindly about an abstract force or entity, but to love life in all of its different forms. This means that we should love not only the strong, the vibrant, the healthy, the wealthy, the charming and the beautiful, but that we should also love and respect our elders, protect the vulnerable, heal the sick, feed the hungry, assist the homeless, clothe the naked, cultivate those who are coarse and or ugly, and, nurture the young and ignorant.

We should also gather together to worship God with love, not with grand words. Which means that as individuals we should engage in spiritualising our lives through both Prayer and Meditation; that we should do no violence to people or to the creatures of the world; that we should covet neither person nor thing; that we should minimise our aspirations for wealth, status, power, authority and control. Furthermore, it means that we should speak the truth or, remain silent.

These very potent ways of modifying our behavioural reflexes, our *habitus*, are expressed in the way we organise our lives. Such ways are easy enough when they coincide with

37   c.f. Matt. 6: 33 'seek ye first the kingdom of God'.
38   Luke 17: 21
39   Luke 10:27

our natural inclinations, but they can be difficult when we are confronted with a conflict of interests. Consequently, we are encouraged as Order members, to develop the civic virtues of Prudence, Fortitude, Justice and Temperance. These four ancient modes of behaviour determine how we can view and engage with life.

The virtue of *prudence* is concerned with making informed decisions and managing resources wisely. To be able to do this effectively applies to both the individual and the community, as good management of people and resources contributes towards individual well-being and communal harmony and prosperity. It is all-inclusive. The virtue of *fortitude*, by which is meant courage, is concerned with bearing hardship and discomfort patiently and with humility, especially as life is so unpredictable and full of pitfalls and obstacles. However, it is not simply about bravery, but also about recognising and striving after that which is noble and good, about turning away from all that is base and unworthy – that takes courage!

The virtue of *temperance*, is concerned with controlling the excesses of the carnal nature, excesses which take many forms, but in the end they all derive from desire. We must learn to guard against them, setting appropriate limits to the wanderings of the discursive mind, for if our carnal nature is left unchecked it will fill the imagination with desires that are fanciful if not foolish. The virtue of *justice* is concerned with ordering and managing our lives in such a way that we can live in harmony with our fellows; maintaining the principle of dealing in an even-handed manner with all. This may seem to be simple and in many ways obvious; however, the theory is one thing, applying it is another.

So far, the virtues have been described in the context of defining and shaping the individual's role in society. As such they are known as the 'civic' virtues for they facilitate the socialising of the individual and the consequent evolution of civilisation. In that process they are concerned with the development of reason and the moderation of our passionate nature. Thus, we learn to control appetites, manage resources and order our lives in harmony with our fellows. Yet, there is a great deal more to the virtues than civic development, they are a central component of the spiritual potential residing within each one of us. Consider, for instance, the development of prudence: the discursive mind learns the art of reasoning, by which resources are managed wisely and the excesses of the carnal nature are controlled. This leads to the art and discipline of meditation, in which the reasoning powers evolve, learning to engage in pure spiritual thought.

In principle, it is the art of managing internal resources, albeit on another level. It is the same with the other virtues. Fortitude for example, begins with learning to accept hardship and control aggression. However, it also extends into learning how to overcome fear, particularly the very human fear of being alone, of being rejected by the herd as it were, for standing up for our values as we seek that which is noble, and more pertinently, overcome the fear of being separated from established comfort zones. With temperance, the soul begins to control appetite and passion, eventually learning how to transcend and sublimate the passionate nature, whereby desire is transformed into empathy and passion is transformed into compassion. Whereas, in developing a sense of justice, the soul learns how to order its life according to the law of the land and live in harmony with its fellows. Thus, we are led in our prayer-life by the Holy Spirit, along an ascending spiral of virtue, into a state of stillness and peace that is beyond all other human experience. It is a peace that mankind can neither give nor take away. This is the beginning of contemplation through which we are gradually assimilated into the spiritual life and where we begin to accomplish our true function, for 'the goal of the virtuous life is likeness to the Divinity'[40].

The cultivation of the virtues is, then, important both in the life of the individual and socially. For those who are destined to have a role in the Church hierarchy there are other things to be taken into consideration. Although Order members are not expected to take major orders, for those who do, some knowledge of Order disciplines and studies is expected. Additional subjects, such as, Liturgical Studies, The Sacraments, Apostolic Church History and Free Church Denominations are among the those that require study.

---

40   Hall, Stuart George (trans.), *Gregory of Nyssa, Homilies on the Beatitudes*, Brill, Leiden 2000.

Context

It appears to be generally true that following every disaster or trauma, such as a war, plague, drought or earthquake, there is an awakening of interest in occultism and esoteric thought. Perhaps this is simply a social release valve that allows people to exorcise the horrors they had experienced, to make sense of the mindless and senseless barbarities they had witnessed. On the other hand the uncertainties presented by such events do focus the mind upon things that would otherwise be 'swept under the carpet'.

In returning to the period in question – 1948 to 1955 – it is important to recall what was actually going on in the world. Clearly, the world was recovering from a very nasty war. My memories of the early 1950's are few, I was, after all, born in 1951, but I do remember a country working feverishly to return to some degree of normality. Bomb-sites were still common-place, as were gas-lighting and outside toilets. Water was often acquired from external stand-pipes; and rationing was in force until 1953/4. War had beggared the country; the NHS was in its infancy; there was little 'social security', and housing, together with its furniture, and many of the basics were difficult to obtain. Society and communities had been fragmented and the loss of people, through death, injury and displacement devastated communities. I do not exaggerate when I say that poverty and uncertainty was the norm for most people!

Furthermore, the Church, rightly or wrongly, had been perceived to have let the country down. Why? Perhaps the truth is simply that the Church was an 'easy' target. Whatever the reasons, people needed something more substantial than pious words, noble gestures and fine platitudes, so it should come as no surprise that the interest in the 'psychic' and 'spiritual' worlds was stronger than ever before. Many people, their psyches' fragmented by the horrors of war, were desperately trying to re-establish 'order' and 'meaning' in their lives, which was difficult if not impossible in the traditional religious establishments, so people looked elsewhere. Indeed, whatever religious certainty had existed before 1939, had pretty much disappeared by 1945, and little has changed since.

It was precisely here that Mar Georgius could have found a worthwhile platform on which to grow his Church, but as the history-books show, that wasn't to happen. Instead, people wandered from place to place, from teacher to teacher, from school to school, looking for answers to their problems, and there were few in the Church who were able to give them the answers they sought.

Many asked awkward questions, such as, Why Suffering? Or if there was a God, then why did He create all the bad things in Life? Forgetting we create that stuff, not God. If you are asking why does God let it happen? Then wake up! If God controlled everything we would have no free-will and then we would be complaining about that – if we could! However, although we control our own destiny, this does not mean we can avoid all of the ills in the world, because when I say 'we' I mean the communal or corporate 'we' – we share our fate jointly, to which we individually contribute our share of stuff. So, if we communally allow our water to be poisoned; allow our foods to be contaminated; allow our air to be polluted; allow our fish-stock to be depleted, allow our land to be owned and our food to be controlled, through corporate greed and ambition, then we will share in the fall-out. It is as simple as that. Furthermore, if we allow greedy, ambitious, vain and conceited sociopaths to control our lives and to lead us into wars, then we will suffer the consequences. Stop blaming God, grow-up, take some responsibility, do something about it and move on!

Which brings me to the Order of Dionysis & Paul. As discussed at the beginning, we appear to consist of two contrary natures and we never really know which one will rule the day. To recap, the first is reactionary, an instinctive nature that responds to experience on a like/dislike basis. The second is a rational creature who is either a slave or the master of its appetites, dreams, desires and aspirations. The primary objective of the Order is the transformation of this dual nature, this base metal of human behaviour, into the gold of Spiritual understanding.

For most people, it appears to be the case that they are reasonably happy with the secular world – and we do well to remember that the Order of Dionysis & Paul is not for them – however, for some, who have felt the inner prompting that is incomprehensible to those who have not felt it, they can do nothing else but begin the journey. One thing is certain about that beginning, each of those who begin will start from a place of spiritual darkness, from which they will move gradually towards a place of light and understanding. They might rush, they might dawdle, and occasionally they will push themselves beyond their limited understanding, taking many wrong turnings in the process, but they will begin. It is to such people the Order speaks and to whom this small book is addressed!

There are different ways to describe the work of the Order, each of which have limitations in expression, and at different times many have been used. But it is important because without understanding what it does and why it does so, little sense will be made of its existence. I have used one way to describe the work, using the virtues and *habitus* to describe what is involved. The development of virtue is a tried and tested model that speaks of the transforming power of sustained intention, and transforming our *habitus* describes what we must do to achieve the goal. Another way speaks of it being accomplished in four phases that divide naturally into two parts. The first can be described as the preliminary or Outer Work and the second as more advanced Inner Work.

The Outer Work consists firstly of: *Purification,* which is the laborious process of extracting the Will from the controlling influence of the lower or instinctive nature. I have already described some of what is involved in this work in the previous pages, so I shall be brief. The concept of changing one's *habitus* is central to this work, but that is only partly in our gift to change, the major part of the work of sublimating our established *habitus* is the gift of the Holy Spirit.

It is not by any act of spiritual prowess that the goal of sublimating our *habitus* is attained, but through the conscious development of a quiet heart, wherein obedience, tranquillity, and a willingness to serve others, enables the soul to grow. Those who develop such qualities do not vaunt themselves above others but follow the example of the Lord, who took the lowly form of a man, and instead of living in regal majesty chose the simple life of a tradesman's son. At the heart of such meekness is the willingness to serve God and to serve the common good without any desire to serve oneself; for humility is best attained through the sublimation of 'self' in duty. Humility becomes then an outward expression of an inner stillness, a stillness that has taken the place of the incessant mental chatter of a mind dominated by the world of the senses. Such a state denotes the proper disposition of a soul aspiring to live in the 'Presence' of God. Thus, *purification*, is a cleansing of 'self-hood' through service to God and the greater good.

Secondly: *Elevation*, which is accomplished by the refining of the Will through spiritual disciplines and raising the emerging consciousness along the 'middle way'. The most effective means available to accomplish this is prayer, because in prayer we are prepared for the reception of the gift of Grace, which elevates and conforms our will to the Will of God. It is the mould into which the volatile chemistry of our consciousness is poured, and the means by which we can open the doorway of the sanctuary within the hidden temple of the heart. It has been treasured by spiritual aspirants from the earliest times, for prayer has its own special teacher in God. Without it, spiritual development can only take place at a mundane pace which means, slowly, very slowly.

This leads us into the heart of Order life. Prayer, in its most dynamic form is achieved through ritual, such as the celebration of the Eucharist or the daily offices. The gathering of the Order to celebrate the Eucharist, to engage in meditation or other related activities is fundamental to the communal life and wellbeing of the Order, and is therefore obligatory upon all members. Such activity also provides the opportunity to break bread together, to exchange and discuss topical and local news, and to engage in fruitful spiritual and philosophical discussion.

It is common practice for the members to breakfast together after the celebration of the Eucharist, during which the readings of the day are discussed and local news shared, bringing members up to date with current affairs as they relate to the Order. This practice is generally continued when members gather for other services such as the Evening Office or Compline. On such occasions a group discussion invariably takes place concerning relevant subjects, such as the understanding of a passage of scripture or the significance of a spiritual experience.

The Order also gathers together on a regular basis to discuss spiritual and philosophical matters as outlined in the curriculum. These events normally take place in the evening, after an office. Such occasions are treated as on-going seminars where instruction is given on matters of the curriculum. Less frequently, members gather for a day long seminar on a specific subject. All of the aforementioned applies to the outer development of the soul – the development of a new *habitus*, which is, arguably, never fully accomplished, but it is often achieved sufficiently on earth for the purpose of a soul's life in the service of God.

It is, then, to this labour that the Inner Work applies. Such work consists of *Sacrifice,* by which is meant the surrender of the Will to the Logos, our Lord Jesus Christ, who may require of us a quiet life of prayer and meditation; of writing; or of teaching. Alternatively, what the Lord may require need not be complex or transcendental. For example, we may be an accomplished musician destined for great things, yet against all logic we may be asked to surrender our ambitions, to work with the sick, either in mind or body, to serve the poor, or to labour in distant lands. As it is written, "The harvest truly is great, but the labourers are few,"[41] and the 'cure of souls' is a never-ending task with many variations.

Finally, *Consecration,* which is the transformation of the purified Human Will in its union, or Celestial marriage, with the Divine Logos, known to Christians as the Lord Jesus Christ. In this final part of the work, the soul itself is transformed. Individuals may remain serving wherever they are, but the transformation is complete. The new birth has been accomplished and little of value can be said about it here!

---

41   Luke 10:2

It is obvious that evangelising and pastoral work does not form a major part of the Order's life, but this does not mean that it is discounted or dismissed. Arguably the best form of evangelising is not preaching at people, but living the Christian life for all to see; engaging with people quietly and with kindness, treating them as we may want to be treated. From this type of behaviour pastoral work extends naturally — *this is the best form of evangelising!* It may or may not be our place to run a soup kitchen, to feed the hungry and clothe the naked etc. It may be that it is sufficient to contribute a part of our income to the relevant charities that do such work, but whatever we do, it should not be done in lieu of our own spiritual work, but as a part of it.

We might also ask ourselves and others, how is it that so many people are in need today; how is it there are so many homeless, hungry and sick people living in the world? If we are honest with ourselves, we may not like the answer!

Allan Armstrong

In 1988 Mar Francis consecrated Allan Armstrong as Bishop Marcus, to continue the work of the Holy Celtic Church. When Bishop Marcus undertook the administration of the Church and the Order, he recognised that Mar Francis had accomplished most of what he set out to do — he had established the Order within the Holy Celtic Church, and it was now free to engage in the spiritual life on its own terms. Mar Francis had

Fig. 19. Bp Marcus

also provided the Church with continuity in passing on the episcopacy to Bp Marcus. What was still lacking was an 'upper-room' free from the domestic environment. To achieve this thing was one of Bishop Marcus' first tasks. A task which presented some surprising results.

It transpired that one of the members of the Order, Br John, owned some properties, one of which, a small cottage on Shellards Lane, Alveston, Near Thornbury, South Gloucestershire, was empty and needed work doing to it. He offered it to the Order on favourable terms so we (the Order) set about fixing it up. On the ground floor, the main room was arranged as a meeting room with the kitchen and toilet facilities adjacent. Upstairs, the largest room was transformed into an oratory with a small vestry adjacent. The cottage was far from perfect, but what was ideal about it was that it was a detached building free of all domestic activity, which meant that members could stay without inconveniencing anyone. On Holy Saturday, the 10th of April 1993, the oratory of the Holy Cross was duly consecrated, and made ready for the midnight service of 'bringing in' the New Fire. It was a fitting climax to months of work by members of the Order.

One of the saddest duties that arose early in Bp Marcus' administration, concerned the Lincoln community. Bp Eric's health was failing and on the 14th of May 1993, the Rev Martin

Betty Eades - died at Foxby Hill Nursing Home Lincolnshire - 11th May 2017 aged 87 years. (wife of Eric Eades)

The Learning Curve

Fig.20. Eric & Heather

Eric had been suffering with cancer for some years, and had undergone many surgical operations to halt or slow down its progress. When they arrived in Lincoln it was clear that the end was near, and after consulting the medics it was thought best to administer the last rites without delay. They also deconsecrated Eric's private oratory on the same visit, and on Tuesday the 18th of May, at 2am, the Rt Reverend Eric Eades died in St. Barnabas Hospice, Lincoln. A Requiem Mass was celebrated on his behalf by members of the Order.

The community of St Gregory Palamas, which Eric had formed and dedicated to healing, and which he ran for some years, was now without its guiding light in Lincoln. His Deacon, Heather Woods, an Associate Member of the ODP, remained to administer to the flock, but unfortunately, Heather died later that year. It was intended that a priest from Bristol would visit monthly to administer the sacraments, however, because of her death this did not happen.

It was reported by her family and friends that Heather, who was also afflicted with cancer, had been receiving high doses of morphine for some time, and that her medication had been withdrawn, leaving her 'desolate and in agony.' In this tortured state, she took her own life by throwing herself in the river. What is curious about this report about her death is that according to other reports, Heather was not denied the pain-relief she required[42] and, in any case she was unable to walk, thus, presumably, unable to walk to the river.

Heather's life was, so it seemed at the time, to be a series of connected and interlinked, yet unique episodes. For example, in 1992, Heather had been admitted into a hospice in Lincoln as the end of her life was thought to be near. As Bp Marcus remembers it, during one discussion about this, she informed him that:

Fig. 21. Heather Woods

> "When I was in the hospice, I had an experience. I knew that I would not die, that I had work to do. After a night's sleep I woke up feeling well, I was brighter than I had been for months, and I began to eat. I came off the morphine and was walking again. My hair has begun to re-grow remarkably fast and healthy, and my skin glowed with vitality."

Heather also informed him that she walked out of the hospice, apparently healthy, and returned to her life of healing. How long this lasted is unknown, but clearly, at some point in time the cancer returned and a new episode began wherein pain-management was a priority.

Heather was also blessed, or cursed if you will, with *Stigmata* – a term that describes a physical manifestation upon a person's body of the bleeding wounds of Christ's passion (hands, feet, head and side). Many think of Stigmata as a sign of special holiness, others have a different view. In Heather's case it was something of both, on the one hand, together with the *Stigmata* came a state of blessedness and peace, but on the other hand came the envy, the doubts and the negative outbursts of those who were not really party to her life. There were also many visions and 'inspired writings'. These had occurred previously, without the *Stigmata*, but they were given a fresh impetus by

---

42   Records, 3. p. 16.

it, and were interlinked thematically in many instances. A very interesting account of this is given in *Spirit Within Her* by John and Anne Spencer.[43]

Stigmata is not a recent phenomenon. The first reported case was St Francis of Assisi; he acquired *Stigmata* in 1224, two years before his death. John and Anne Spencer estimate more than 300 cases of *Stigmata* have been recorded since the time of St. Francis, by far the majority being women. Views are mixed about the nature and occurrence of this phenomenon, but Heather's experience is of particular interest because it is one of the best documented cases in history, and no doubts about it have ever been suggested. Heather died[44] on November 21-22, 1993, a few months after the death of bishop Eric Eades.

Eric had been ordained by Mar Francis on December the third 1983, for the community in Lincoln, and on Pentecost Sunday, 22nd of May 1988, he had been consecrated as a bishop of the Holy Celtic Church, again to serve the community he was building up in Lincoln, especially with regards to healing – harking back to the objectives of the Order, set out in 1948[45].

The loss of a caring and busy community in Lincoln through Eric and Heather's demise was a sad event in the history of the Order. However, there was little that could be done, as the community in and around Bristol was either too old and retired, or were too young and inexperienced. Most of its members were just beginning, and were as yet unqualified to function in the cauldron that was Lincoln. Furthermore, Bp Eric had left no clear paper-trail or *modus-operandi* for the Bristol Community to follow. Consequently, those who were left in Lincoln were dealt a double blow by the deaths of Eric and Heather from which they never recovered.

However, not all was bad news for the Order. The Bristol Community was growing and the Record Book shows an ongoing development of the Order as members passed through the minor orders. Bp Marcus, also recognised that things needed to change.

---

43   Published by, Boxtree Ltd., London, 1994. ISBN: 9781852834968
44   The nature of her death made the precise time of her death uncertain.
45   See the Notice on p. 16.

Fig. 22. Digging up the floor

The chapel at Alveston could only seat so many people (10+) and we regularly had 20+ people attend. The Order was fast approaching the limits of the chapel of the Holy Cross. A larger chapel was needed. An opportunity emerged when Br John, offered the Order the long-term use of a run-down barn located several hundred yards from the Holy Cross chapel. Br John had inherited a small farm of 150 acres, but with many derelict farm-buildings within its curtilage. The barn was one of those buildings. A lot of work was needed to make the barn usable, including taking out approximately two feet of concrete floor to provide sufficient height. Work

Fig. 23. Moving the compressor

began on Wednesday 12 July 1995. The floor was excavated, which took some days and a lot of hard work to accomplish, then a gas-fired under-floor heating system was installed. With the floor thus far prepared the Order was able to proceed according to plan. Fund-raising was central to the enterprise, as the Order was not, indeed never has been blessed with disposable income. Through various fund-raising endeavours, such as donations, Jumble sales, art-sales and a sponsored walk between Bristol and Bath, sufficient funds were raised to finish the job. If my memory serves me well it cost in the region of £10,000, and more than six months' labour to realise

Fig. 24. Holy Cross Chapel

this project. Almost all of the unskilled labour was provided free of charge by Order members. On Tuesday the 6th February the first chapel of the Holy Cross was closed down in preparation for the consecration of the new chapel of the Holy Cross, which took place on Saturday, the 6th April 1996. The new chapel, which could seat 20+ was an immediate success. During the consecration of the new chapel, Bp Marcus was given inspiration with regards to the ordination of women priests. This was duly noted and acted upon, and the Order now has five women priests in its ranks.

The curriculum was another matter, it is more complex and time-consuming – indeed it is a life's work. It is possible to teach people relatively quickly to be adept in many subjects, without them learning anything that is spiritually essential or important, furthermore, as valuable as they might be, the training of Graduates, Doctors and Professors is not, in truth, what the Lord incarnated and suffered for.

A major feature of the new chapel of the Holy Cross was a larger vestry and a separate changing room for Order members. As time passed, another part of the building was developed to accommodate a conference and meeting room that could, and occasionally did seat sixty plus people. Unfortunately, the situation went to Br John's head and he took it upon himself to act as if his generosity gave him the right to be an autocratic teacher to the Order. Things became heated as members reacted against his presumption, and eventually, in 2003, the Order withdrew from the premises and on the 1st February 2004, Brother John resigned. Lessons were being learned by a new generation of members about the self-serving nature of the first Adam!

With regard to Prayer & Meditation, the core teachings had been addressed, and it had long been recognised that they will evolve as times and places change, but changing the '*habitus*' of a new member requires constant attention, because it is a new and unique process for every member who engages with it. Furthermore, without humility, the capacity and willingness to change will always be very difficult; indeed, it has been the 'immovable object' within the heart of those members of the Order who have resigned, and probably will remain so in the future.

The question remains, how does a contemplative order maintain a spiritual discipline that modifies one's *habitus*? The expectations have always been that a member aspires to engage in the Offices thrice daily – upon rising, at noon and before retiring – and join in meetings twice a week. Regular studies are encouraged as and when the opportunity presents itself. However, this is not really a change of *habitus*. The mindfulness necessary for genuine *habitus* transformation requires a 24/7 conscious engagement. This may be possible when approached as a religious or philosophical exercise, but highly unlikely, because without an attentive mind and the input of the Holy Spirit, a change in *habitus* is not possible. It is, I believe, true to say that the attention necessary for a change of *habitus* is generally lost in a never ending state of mental and emotional flux, and without the disciplines of Prayer & Meditation to focus the attention, and to stabilise the chemistry of consciousness, the ability to change the *habitus* remains out of the question.

Yet, this is not the problem it first appears to be. It is not simply a question of opportunity and right conditions. Neither does everyone have the luxury of retiring to a monastery or a retreat, and even if they did, it would make little difference. People do need to work, to attend to domestic affairs, to engage with the world, with family and friends if they are to survive. Thus, it is not so much what is done as how it is done. We must spiritualise our life in its entirety if we are to change our behavioural reflexes.

The early Church, especially in the first few centuries, found its strength not only *in the Lord*, but also by *emulating the Lord*. This is what is meant by the term 'exemplar'. The Lord Jesus Christ is the model, the antitype of our aspirations and we really must engage with that if we are to evolve. For many people today this is difficult to comprehend, yet it is the basis of the spiritual life of the Order, and arguably, it was the basis of the lives of the Desert Communities of the Levant, of the primitive Celtic Church, and of the early monastic settlements of Europe. This is what *habitus* means to the Order. It sets the Order apart, not in an elitist fashion, but in its dedication to the work of spiritual transformation, which has ever been the work of the Church.

On Friday the fourteenth of November 1997, Brother Johanan was initiated into the Order, and on Sunday twenty-first of September 2008, Br Johanan was ordained a priest by Bp Marcus at the Bristol New Church with the purpose of establishing a spiritual community in Cornwall. He began with starting a Meditation Group, and soon found that most of the established "New-Age" and pagan communities were

Fig. 25. Br Johanan

set against his Christian approach, even some of the Christian groups who were established in his area resented his presence. Nevertheless, he persevered and his group continues to flourish. In his own words:

"I think one of the more memorable events from my perspective in Cornwall was developing the meditation group which now flourishes. As an adjunct to the meditation group, several people started to stay behind after the meditation session had finished and asked for healing. At first, it wasn't something that I was confident performing. However, the fact that group members seemed to intuitively gravitate to something I had not officially offered, made me give it a try.

"I remember praying silently asking if I might be used as a channel for the Lord's healing light. I rather nervously held my hands over the recipient's head and just trusted in that higher power to use me as an instrument of healing if that is what was right for the individual recipient. What followed surprised me and caused the recipient to be amazed. Although her eyes were closed she knew exactly where my hands were placed even though I didn't actually touch her or indeed get any closer than an inch or so away from her. From my perspective, I realised that as I moved my hands away from her head, she leaned towards my hands like they were magnets. As I pushed my hands towards her, she moved her head back again. Another group member witnessed the whole thing and sat open mouthed but thankfully, silent.

"I continued to do the same with other members in turn and then we sat for a while in silence. Afterwards the first recipient couldn't contain herself. She said that she felt something coming out of the palms of my hands like they were electric and emitting heat. If I moved my hands she felt herself swaying towards where she perceived them to be. Other members reported experiencing something similar.

"This has been a profound experience for me, especially as these people reported later that their health responded positively. I felt very humbled that I was trusted as an instrument of the Divine. To this day, and each time I offer healing, I am still in awe at the unseen power that underpins all things."

Fig. 26. Dartington Hall

In 1999, it was decided that the Order should host a Conference about the future of the Western Mystical Tradition – a term that means many things to many people, and which was a matter of some debate at the time – during the third Millennium. It was generally agreed that a historical venue that spanned the history of Great Britain would be ideal, and on that note Dartington Hall, in Totnes, Devon was selected. The estate consists of approximately one thousand acres, The current Hall was built at the end of the fourteenth century; it is a remarkable example of the architecture of that period.

Dorothy and Leonard Elmhirst bought the estate in 1925 and embarked on what they called the Dartington Experiment to regenerate a rural community. The Elmhirsts welcomed artists, economists, horticulturists and social reformers to Dartington and encouraged them to grapple with the pressing issues of their day. The common theme then, as now, concentrated on making the world a better place for others. Today Dartington is a social enterprise that ploughs the surplus from its commercial enterprises back into the many projects they fund and support.

Here in October 1999, the Future of the Western Mystery Tradition Conference, as it entered the new millennium, took place over three days. The conference presented a variety of papers dealing with the different elements of the Tradition as understood by the various scholars who took part. The papers were interspersed with structured discussions directly related to the lectures. From the lectures, discussions and a general forum, a considered statement was to be formulated, setting out how the Western Mystical Tradition might best fulfil its role in the Third Millennium. At the heart of the Conference, the Order celebrated the Eucharist, which was attended by the majority of the delegates. The ceremonial form of the Eucharist was overtly mystical and it greatly moved those present. The Conference was a memorable event that was well attended by people from many different parts of the globe.

On Sunday 11ᵗʰ June, 2000, a wedding service was held at Gara Rock, Devon. The blessed couple had chosen the spot, and having first fulfilled a secular wedding service in the Gara Rock Hotel, came to the beach for a spiritual wedding service. The setting was, without overstating the facts, breathtaking and

Fig. 27. Wedding at Gara Rock, Devon, 2000

timeless. The weather was absolutely perfect, blue skies, sunshine and a warm light breeze, and the bride, cloaked in royal blue, wearing a floral head-dress of laurel leaves, gypsophila and roses, accompanied by the groom, cloaked in a dawn-grey cloak and sporting a head-dress of laurel leaves, looked every bit like Saxon nobility. Bp Marcus was the celebrant, assisted by members of the Order. After the service, champagne was served and the festivities began; they continued until the evening, when the elders retired and the young went on to more fun, befitting a wedding.

Fig. 28. Bristol New Church

However, life is more than fun and games, and the move from the chapel of the Holy Cross, Alveston, was developing apace. A fortuitous meeting with Dr Bob Gilbert led to the idea of sharing a building with the Bristol Society of the New Church. The New Church is the name given to the organisation that follows the teachings of Immanuel Swedenborg, the eighteenth century Swedish visionary and scientist. As a result of that meeting, Bp Marcus and Sr Rachael met with the leadership of the Church over the period of a year or so, and in due course a license was granted giving the Order permission to share their space.

Thus, on Christmas Eve 2003, members of the Bristol Society of the New Church came together with members of the Holy Celtic Church, to share a carol service and to sign jointly an agreement for eighteen months use, with the option to renew. The agreement was signed by Bp Marcus for the Holy Celtic Church and John Lewin for the New Church.[46]

Because the Holy Celtic Church is essentially catholic, Trinitarian and sacramental, a portable chapel that could be set up and dismantled had to

Fig. 29. Portable Chapel

46   Record Vol. 3, p. 85

be designed, as the Church's ceremonial is very different from that of the New Church. The Order also hosted a series of seminars in the Bristol New Church. The seminars were designed as an introduction to the Tradition, and covered subjects such as the nature of the Soul, Spiritual Hierarchies and Ritual & Ceremonial. They were designed to be inter-active, to inform the listener, and to involve as many of the Order as possible in the running of them. The seminars were well received. The Order also began video recording these events with some degree of success, although it is true to say that without professional editing they are only good for archival purposes.

The seminars were very well attended considering they were private events that were not advertised and open only to members of the Order, the Fellowship and friends. The average turnout was thirty-five plus people. The events were a success thanks to the efforts of Br Luke, & Sr Sophia, who helped to make the seminars at the New Church work. The Order also ran a series of experiments in teaching Meditation. These experiments were conducted in public, with mixed results. The implications were significant, indeed, what became patently obvious was that a very different approach was needed than had gone before.

In the years that the Order spent sharing with the New Church, relations with their community were always open and friendly. However, they were an aging community, and like many Christian congregations all over Europe, they were losing members far more quickly than they could replace them. With economic forces being dominated by politics, money and cash-flow, the Order's future was tenuous at the New Church; furthermore, the process of assembling and taking apart the chapel was becoming a little wearing. Thus, during the annual Synod of 2010 it was agreed that the Order's time at the New Church had reached its conclusion, and that it should move to the newly established chapel at Wick.

This decision was also based upon the understanding that the move to Wick would be temporary, and furthermore, enable the Order to fund-raise more effectively, with a view to purchasing a property suitable for its needs. With awareness-

Contemporary celtic poems
read by their authors and set to music

Fig. 30. Oratio Album Cover

raising in mind the Order produced audio recordings of the *Glastonbury Mass 1984*, *Compline* and the *Morning Office*, which can be heard on their website: *www.ecclesiasticaceltica.org*, (see also the online magazine the *Fellowship Herald*). The Order also recorded various members reading their own spiritual poems and prayers. These were set to music and a CD was produced with a view to fund-raising.

In July 2012, after much planning and preparation, Srs Phoebe and Mary began a weekly meditation course. It has evolved as one would expect and, is now well established and known as the FDP[47] South Gloucester Meditation group. Because of work commitments Sr Mary withdrew, and for the last five years it has been run by Sr Phoebe. In August 2017 the group moved from Wick to Emersons

Fig. 31. Sr Phoebe

Green, South Glos – there is a better public transport network, making the new venue more accessible for people. In her own words:

"The meditation group welcomes people from all backgrounds and beliefs who are interested in learning how to meditate using very practical tried and tested methods. People come from various walks of life and for various reasons and it would seem that many people want different outcomes from meditation. In the first session we discuss reasons why people seek to meditate, here are some examples:

'To learn about meditation in a supportive and compassionate environment; to seek peace and calmness;

47   Fellowsip of Dionysis & Paul

to learn ways to reduce stress; to learn how to relax; to lower blood pressure; to be able to discuss spiritual matters freely; and to learn how to silence negative, destructive thoughts'. At first, very few mention a spiritual journey, but by the time the six week induction course is finished, a number of people find themselves eagerly seeking just that.

The induction course, which lasts for six or seven weeks, starts with an introduction to the breathing and relaxation exercises, followed by exercises in imagination culminating in therapeutic meditation. Gradually, over the duration of the course, the student becomes more familiar and proficient with their breathing, relaxation and concentration. With the more advanced group, there is a mixture of teaching, reading from the scriptures and meditation. In due course, students are introduced to therapeutic meditation and Lectio Divina.

Some aspects of the teaching are repeated from time to time. Many students say that they are grateful for this, because there is so much to learn at the beginning and they easily forget. Also, I believe their understanding evolves over time and they hear things in a different way. The regular students are demonstrating a steady and deeper understanding of the spiritual mysteries, and all have reported positive changes in their everyday lives. It is a great privilege to have the opportunity to share what I feel is my limited knowledge in this field and I am also learning so much through them."

About the same time, the *Oratio Project* – an online fund-raising initiative, designed to raise the funds necessary to build the first of a network of dedicated spiritual houses, that would facilitate a new model of monasticism, was conceived and implemented at Wick. It was partly successful in that it did raise some funds and also raised awareness, but it was not the Order's best effort. In its defence, it must be said that the understanding of organising and managing an online fundraising event, such as the *Oratio Project*, was insufficient, and with hind-sight needed more research and support.

Srs Phoebe and Sophia, worked with Brs James and Andrew to produce a short video to promote the *Oratio Project*. And still on the theme of digital technology, Br Luke spent many hours editing the Zoom Fellowship material, which is available online as a resource for all members to peruse. Brother Johanan, who had been running a meditation group in Bude for some years, apart from designing and managing our website, *www.ecclesiasticaceltica.org*, also developed a Facebook Page to present the Order work in Cornwall. Overall, things were progressing quite well.

In 2012, Bp Marcus and Sr Rachael, with the help of Paul Hutchinson, a solicitor of the Memorial Woodlands Ltd, who was well known to Bp Marcus in that connection, and who also specialised in establishing charities, started proceedings to register the Holy Celtic Church as a charity. After months of negotiations, the constrictions that were imposed by the Charities Commission, although understandable, were too much for the Order to bear at that time, and the application was withdrawn by Bp Marcus.

Fig. 32. Sr Rachael

Also, Bp Marcus and Sr Rachael had sought for some time to establish a financial accounting system for the Order, but with increasing frustration. Banking regulations seemed to be set against 'group' accounts unless they were a registered Limited Company, or conformed to rigid stereotypes, none of which were suitable. Eventually, a Company Limited by Guarantee was seen as the best option and registered in the name of Ecclesiastica Celtica Ltd, which in effect operates as a mutual society. The Holy Celtic Church is now administered through this company. Sr Hannah, the Bursar, looks after the accounts, overseen by the Committee of Synod, thereby keeping everything as it should be.

As events transpired, the move to Wick was something of a mixed blessing. The chapel, a converted barn/workshop that had been restored under the supervision of Sr Rachael, was delightful. It was entered through a vestry/kitchen area and was light warm and airy. It could seat 20+ people comfortably, with additional space that had been converted into studios, and these were also available at need for meetings etc. At first all was well, there was a good harmony among the brethren. However, Wick had been made too comfortable and too cosy, a condition that lends itself to *Accidie* (spiritual apathy). Members began to lose sight of their primary objective, which is to follow the Path, to sublimate themselves in the Lord, and to study the Tradition.Instead some members began to elevate the 'self' at Wick, which was to have

ramifications later on. To understand the significance of this, it is important to recognise that the Order practises a form of silence – to speak only when spoken to and then to answer only if necessary or appropriate[48] – so that its members can maintain the inner life without engaging in secular or frivolous distractions. Idle talk or gossip is also frowned upon as it generally elevates

Fig. 33. Wick Chapel

'self' at someone else's expense. These basic principles of the Rule were gradually being eroded at Wick as some of the members started to look around them and make secular and personal judgements. It is tempting to go into some detail about this, but there are already enough testimonies written about the damage that can be done when members of a religious or monastic order begin to act in such a way, making it unnecessary for me to cite further examples.[49]

Nevertheless, the writing was on the wall, and in 2016 the Wick chapel was closed down and the members reverted to their own oratories. This proved to be a timely and cathartic process in which, slowly but surely, a great healing began as the members busied themselves establishing and refining their own oratories. Sr Sophia refurbished the top floor of her home to accommodate an oratory and a vestry and meeting-room. Sr Phoebe did likewise in that she re-organised her oratory to suit her expanding needs. Bp Matthias re-arranged his oratory, and his diary to accommodate others, as did Sr Claudia. Bp Marcus installed a garden-room that was converted into an oratory in which ten+ people could

48   ODP Rule, part Five, p. 7
49   See *Paradise of the Fathers,* by Wallis Budge

sit with ease. Br James also established an oratory in his garden, sufficient for him to complete his offices. Bp Marcus had set aside six months for this process of adjustment, but in reality it was closer to a year before the *Accidie* and resentment faded away. What was immediately noticeable was the way people stopped judging each other and engaged in the work at hand – discussing instead, who could help who, or how others could be helped.

Sadly, on Sunday the 10th of May, 2015, Sr Rachael died unexpectedly (An abdominal aortic aneurysm, I believe), whilst preparing for Mass. As fate would have it, Order members were on site and the Last Rites were adminstered by Sr Claudia. Her untimely death came as a shock to Order members, and she will be sorely missed. The question goes begging, whatever next? For twenty years and more the Order had sought a home that could serve as a modern form of monastic environment, but it was clearly not what the Holy Spirit wanted. At every turn the aspiration for such an environment has been thwarted, with the simple house-church being presented time and again as the viable option. It remains to be seen what will emerge in the future, but it is reasonably certain that house-churches will be at the heart of any development – radiating from regional centres such as defined by the Oratio Project.

One observation slowly emerged during the Order's time at the Bristol New Church, and became more significant at Wick, members of the Order were no longer centred in one location, town or city, which had, in the main, been the traditional way of things. The membership base was now spread out over a much larger area, as were the people who expressed a general interest in the subject. This meant that regular gatherings in one location became increasingly unfeasible, and although the possibility of running a seminar/conference in one place still remained, regular communal activity required another approach. Furthermore, it was becoming clear that the internet, rather than a reference book or magazine, was the first place that people went to learn about something. With this dawning realisation, the Order gradually began to make changes to the traditional methods of interacting with the world at large.

The Internet was gradually being recognised as a vehicle that could provide some assistance with this, insofar as it is a universal platform that is public and open to the world. Thus, after much discussion through 2011-12, the website *www.ecclesiasticaceltica.org*, was eventually designed and completed by Br Johanan in Cornwall, and is currently maintained by him. However, running regular face-to-face meetings was an increasing problem. The pace of life in the third millennium had increased, and continues to increase without remorse. With the best will in the world people were finding it difficult to sustain long-term commitments to regular evening events. This was answered, in part, by the advances in video conferencing that were being developed on the internet. Like many such organisations, the Order began looking for a video-conference tool that was both understandable by the organisation, and manageable by the public user. There are without doubt some very elegant and sophisticated tools available, but having the understanding, the resources and the depth of pocket to use them is another matter. Nevertheless, the Order did need to engage with something of this sort, but what?

In 2015 the Order began using Skype, as it was relatively accessible and inexpensive to work with, and as they had no idea of what might, or might not, be possible, they boldly stepped forth. However, they soon discovered that although Skype is a very nice tool to use on a small scale, it was still limited in its capabilities; furthermore, it crashed too often, which was frustrating. The Order then tried Webex, which was thought to be the leader in the field, but it was discovered that although it may have been true some years previously, it wasn't so in 2015/16. In short it hadn't been updated for quite a while and it misbehaved terribly.

Eventually the Order was led to Zoom, which provides the most stable platform with a wide range of products the Order might use. As of January 2018, Zoom remains the video-conferencing tool of choice. In spite of the technological developments taking place, new problems began to emerge concerning how to engage with the public on the internet. Apart from displaying information about our vision and mission, about our activities, our objectives, values and aspirations, how can we identify and select members? It is a question that has no easy answer, especially for a contemplative Order such as ours. Looking to increase numbers is a problem; a few souls that are 'ready' are preferred over many that are not, but to acquire those few, many have to be tried, as it is said in other quarters: 'you have to kiss a lot of frogs before you find a prince', and it is a two-way process, individual seekers are just as cautious as any organisation. It takes something special to earn a persons trust online. The question remains, as yet, unanswered.

Nevertheless, the life of the Order remains vibrant and healthy, even though it evolves slowly, as one would expect. For example, Br Matthias had looked to develop a personal liturgical calendar. His expectation was that in a few months it would be sorted, but like all things it was a little more complicated than he anticipated, consequently his research took longer than expected. Furthermore,

Fig. 34. Br Matthias

when he began, Br Matthias had no intention of producing a book out of the material acquired from his research. However, as time passed a book did inevitably emerge. It was completed in 2017 and is now being used throughout the Order. In his own words:

> "It was some years ago, when I began a study of the Liturgical Year of the Church, which is integral to the soul's primary purpose of mystical union with its divine source, our Lord Jesus Christ. One of the issues that emerged from exploring the Church Year was how various important dates and services in some western churches have, over a number of years, fallen into general disuse; perhaps driven by an agenda that has sought to diminish the emphasis of the spiritual life and, replace it with a more simplistic or secular platform.
>
> The Church Year, which in astronomical terms follows the path of the sun, and in spiritual terms follows the life of our Lord Jesus Christ, begins with the first Sunday in Advent, which is the nearest Sunday to St. Andrew's

Day, (30th November). Advent is a time of preparation for the birth of our Lord Jesus Christ following the Winter Solstice, which marks the beginning of the gradual increase in light, warmth and activity.

The Church Year is made up of two cycles which run together from the beginning of the Church Year to its close on the eve of the first Sunday in Advent (Eventide Saturday). These two cycles, the Temporal Cycle and the Sanctoral Cycle, woven together, form the great wheel of the Church Year, and ever present within the centre of this great wheel is the Holy Eucharist, calling the faithful to the true life in our Lord Jesus Christ.

The path of the sun and the lengthening and shortening of days, the winter and summer solstices, the spring and autumn equinoxes, the seasons, the times of the harvests of the earth's bounty, the seeming dormancy of the late autumn and first part of the winter, are all part of an expression of the life of our Lord. Feast days of various saints and services such as Candlemas, Lady Day, May Day and Mary's Month, John the Baptist and Midsummer, Lammas Day, the marking of the end of the Church Year, Plough Sunday and so forth have largely fallen into obscurity and as such so has the sense of the religious life accompanying the rhythm of the seasons, but which is still found in more well-known services such as Harvest Festival.

We have published[50] for our own use some of the notes, prayers, collects and services that we have developed, for the purpose of providing some simple clarity concerning the Church Year, as it unfolds in line with the seasons, establishing a context for the religious life, and the spiritual relationship of every soul with its divine source."

50   *Notes, Prayers, Services & Readings of the Liturgical Year* by Br. Matthias (Bristol, ODP Publications, 2017)

There follows a brief account of the initiations and consecrations that have taken place under Bp Marcus' administration.

Of the sacramental events, such as baptisms, marriages and deaths, and of the many initiations and consecrations, the following are notable. Invariably, all of the following took place during the celebration of the Eucharist.

On Sunday the 7th of June, 1992, Sr Ruth I was initiated. On Friday the 4th of September 1992, Brother Solomon was initiated, and on Friday the 30th of October 1992, Br Lazarus was initiated. All of the above were initiated into the Order by Bp Marcus in the chapel of the Alpha et Omega.

On Friday the 4th of December 1992, Br Matthias was ordained a priest, in the chapel of the Alpha et Omega, by Bp Marcus. On the 11th of April 1993, a Wedding Mass was celebrated by Bp Marcus for Br Lazarus & his wife Sarah, at Holy Cross. On Friday the 30th of July 1993, Sr Ruth II was baptised by Bp Marcus at the chapel of Holy Cross.

On Friday the 19th of November 1993, Sr Sophia I was initiated, on Friday the 19th of August 1994, Sr Ruth II was initiated, and on Friday the 16th of December 1994, Br Francis was initiated. All were initiated by Bp Marcus into the Order at the chapel of Holy Cross.

On Friday the 13th, January 1995, Sr Rachael was initiated into the Order by Bp Marcus. On Friday the 29th September 1995, Br Jacob was initiated into Order by Sr Claudia. On Friday the 6th of September 1997, Sr Mary was initiated into the Order by Bp Marcus. On Friday the 14th of November, 1997, Br Johanan was initiated by Bp Marcus, and on Friday the 1st of May 1998, Sr Phoebe was initiated by Bp Marcus. All of the above were initiated at the chapel of Holy Cross.

On Sunday the 4th of October 1998, Br Solomon was ordained a priest by Bp Marcus. On Friday the 29th of January 1999, Brother Michael was initiated into Order by Bp Marcus, and on Friday the 4th of February 2000, Brother Matthew was initiated into the Order by Bp Marcus. On Sunday the 14th of May 2000, Sr Sophia (Ruth I) was ordained a priest by Bp Marcus. All of the above took place at the chapel of Holy Cross.

On Friday the 26th of October 2001, Br James was initiated into the Order. On Friday the 17th of May 2002, Sr Gabriel was initiated into the Order, both by Bp Marcus at the chapel of Holy Cross, and on Sunday the 18th of August 2002, Br Francis was ordained to the priesthood by Bp Marcus at the chapel of Holy Cross. On the 14th of March 2004, Bp Marcus withdrew the Light and closed the chapel of Holy Cross in Alveston.

On Sunday the 29th of August 2004, Sr Ruth II was ordained a priest by Bp Marcus at the New Church, in Bristol. On Friday the 26th of November 2004, Sr Sarah was initiated by Sr Claudia at the New Church in Bristol. On Sunday the 4th of June, 2006, Sr Phoebe was ordained a priest in the chapel of the New Church, by Bp Marcus. On Friday the 21st of July 2006, Brs Mark & Luke, were initiated into the Order by Bp Marcus at the Bristol New Church. On Friday the 3rd of August 2007, Sr Hannah was initiated into Order by Bp Marcus at the Bristol New Church. On Sunday 21st of September 2008, Br Johanan was ordained a priest by Bp Marcus at the Bristol New Church.

On 19th April, 2009, Brothers Solomon and Matthias were cosecrated to the episcopate at the chapel of the Holy Cross by Bp Marcus, and on Friday 20th July, 2012, at the chapel of the Holy Cross, Wick, Brother Daniel was initiated into the Order by Bp Marcus. On Friday the 21st February, 2014, Sr Elizabeth was initiated into the Order by Bp Marcus, at the chapel of the Holy Cross, Wick. Br Samuel was initiated into the Order by Bp Marcus on Friday 23rd May, 2014, at the chapel of the Holy Cross, Wick. Br Luke was ordained a priest by Bp Marcus on 10th April, 2016 at the chapel of the Holy Cross, Wick, and on the 10th September 2018, Sr Mary was ordained to the priesthood at the chapel of St Raphael, Wiltshire, by Bp Matthias.

The Order today

The Order exists within the Holy Celtic Church. The structure of the community, like that of many religious orders, is based upon degrees of commitment and ability, and consists of Lay-members, (Fellowship members), Novices and Professed members who are dedicated to living the contemplative life whilst dwelling in the secular world. The

Fig. 35. Br Marcus

numerical strength of the Order consists of sixteen professed members, four novices and twenty plus unprofessed members known as 'Fellows', The Order is overseen by four priors who each run their own chapter on a house-church basis. The head of the Order is the Prior-General, currently Brother Marcus.

Until the closure of the Wick chapel in 2016, the community met in person twice weekly. This practice has changed, for reasons already explained, to meeting online on a monthly basis using video-conferencing technology (Zoom). Because of the changes to the way the Order meets, the Fellowship has grown to become more significant and now meets weekly online (Zoom). It was essentially a preparatory school for those beginning to tread the Path, but it is now transforming into something else, the shape of which is not yet clear.

The Order no longer meets in one place but gathers in different oratories for a weekly Eucharist, and comes together for a monthly Eucharist and teaching in the chapel of St Raphael, Swindon. For many years they all lived in the same area (Bristol) and saw each other, often daily, but now they are separated by space and time, nevertheless, the cohesion of the community remains strong and vibrant in spite of the distances that separate them. For this gift we must thank the Formulary, Vow and Rule, which join the members of the Order in equitable bonds of spiritual and communal fraternity. Every member, regardless of status being subject to the same set of standards, and all members being equally bound to act in accordance with them.

The Formulary sets out the basic principles of communal activity within the Order, defining the scope and parameters of engagement for every member – none are exempt. The first requirement is that members of the Order follow the laws of God in Nature, commending all not to be guided by extremes, but to emulate our exemplar – the Lord Jesus Christ; working with all that is wholesome in human nature so that the essential qualities of humanity may be transformed into a new *habitus*.

The head of the Order is the Prior-General, who is both the spiritual and executive head of the Order and its chapters. The general administration of the Order is overseen by a Chapter of senior members. Activities and projects undertaken within the Order are divided into three principal roles: Prior, Co-ordinator, and Operator. Individual members may simultaneously act as a Co-ordinator and an Operator. For example, any member, junior or otherwise, may be requested to organise a seminar; that member then takes the role of Co-ordinator for that undertaking; all other members involved answering to that Co-ordinator, regardless of rank or position. On these terms harmony is maintained within the Order. Every member is expected to stay within the scope of their own activities, thus eliminating cross-currents in the energy of the community. In the pursuit of study all disciplines must be self-motivated as the Order functions more like a college than a nursery school. Guidance and encouragement is always available from senior members but the motivation is self-driven and must come from 'within'.

Furthermore, no member may act as judge or critic of another member. Everyone comes to labour in this field in a state of imperfection, and must be allowed the room to grow and evolve without fear of derision, ridicule or harsh criticism; for who understands the heart of another? Where an irresolvable conflict arises between members, those involved in the conflict are each encouraged to appoint a member of the Order as their representative to negotiate on their behalf until a mutually acceptable settlement is reached.

Many of the Order's day to day activities are orientated towards teaching its members the rudiments of Prayer &

Meditation, and developing the spiritual philosophy and science as outlined in the Order Curriculum. This is done with the expectation that members will use the material to develop an understanding of the first Adam and its *habitus*. Also, prayer has been a central feature of the spiritual life from the earliest times, and was frequently emphasised by the early Church Fathers. So it is with the Order of Dionysis and Paul, in which regularly engaging in prayer is a fundamental part of daily life. Consequently, throughout the day specific times are set aside for prayer so that (a) the soul may recollect itself and persevere in its main purpose – spiritual growth and transformation, and (b) to pray for others, especially the sick and those who find themselves in troubled times.

In 2016, Sr. Sophia delivered two meditation programmes with this objective in mind. However, the situation was more intense than anticipated. The stresses on the working population of our world are becoming increasingly difficult to tolerate as people strive to achieve or maintain living standards that are fast becoming impossible. What set out to be essentially a spiritual objective, became

Fig. 36. Sr Sophia

instead, a remedial workshop for weary souls, worn out bodies and stressed minds. In her own words:

"The first programme was conducted one evening per week as an 'Introduction to meditation' with discussion and practice of simple breath, relaxation and meditation techniques. Those attending came from different walks of life and varied in age from twenty-something to sixty-something. It quickly became obvious that most of those attending were seeking relief from the stresses of secular life; few were consciously looking for spiritual answers, even though it was obvious that most did need to open up the spiritual dimensions of their lives.

The weekly course included learning about the breath and relaxation; the chemistry of stress and its impact upon the body, the emotions, thoughts; and how we translate this in terms of our conduct and behaviour. Individuals in the group gradually started to be able to notice how stress manifested itself upon them in physical emotional and mental terms and the ways in which they either were merely reacting to it or at other times attempting to control stress by slowing down their breathing and practicing the relaxation exercises. One individual who was employed in a very stressful job mentioned that on occasion, when she recalled in memory the meditation group, there was an immediate experience of the feelings of stress literally dissolving away from their body and noticed her emotions calming down.

Part of the programme included becoming aware of impressions made upon mind and body when exposed to certain odours or sounds. During sessions where an essential oil was selected by each person for their meditation – there were a range of experiences reported back to the group. These experiences demonstrated to participants how sensations be they odours, sounds, colours etc can evoke memories and trigger emotional experiences connected to such memories.

All participants expressed that essential oils evoked positive memories; some experienced memories of being with their mother during their childhood and described the experience as seeming as if they had travelled back to that childhood moment. Another person experienced the session in terms of healing and love; and yet another, said they were simply filled with a profound sense of happiness; and yet another found themselves witnessing what they described as a cosmic sunset. In relation to the meditations upon sound – it was reported by one person that their experience of it was like waves; another noticed the sound instantly evoked an image of the sky at night filled with stars.

The second, '*Therapeutic meditation*' is a meditation process guiding participants through a set of breathing, relaxation and visualisation exercises designed to promote the right frame of physical emotional and mental relaxation conducive to healing – an important part of the Order's *raison d'être*.

The most consistent message conveyed by participants attending both these programmes was how easy it was to resist engaging the breathing and relaxation exercises and equally, how readily they felt themselves uplifted in mood and energy when they did make the effort.

Most participants reported increased feelings of improvements in health – from clearing headaches and migraines, to reducing physical aches and the calming of emotion; in one case the complete healing of a long-held spinal injury; and in another the easing of physical discomfort whilst pregnant.

What I observed in running this course is that (a) people have different expectations and very differing experiences of meditation; (b) people respond well to the guided-meditation approach as they find it easier to relax and regulate the breath whilst listening to a gentle voice guiding them; (c) those who grasp and trust the notion that meditation is most effective when regularly practiced will grow spiritually; whilst those who engage only randomly, or only when 'life is getting tricky and harsh', or simply when one 'fancies it' will find meditation an almost fruitless task; (d) most people will struggle to practice the techniques in the early stages and many seem to prefer to practice in a group setting and yet will find that their life circumstances are such that they are ever having to overcome obstacles in order to attend the sessions. This is par for the course and as an ancient wise one once taught, 'perseverance furthers'.

For me, meditation is a labour of love. My plans for future meditation courses include an increased focus on healing, which will hopefully address the modern blight of our working landscape, and make space for spiritual development and mystical experience."

It is a part of Order life that members should pray for others and offer healing to any in need, and that *gratis*. To that end many have dedicated a part of their spiritual life towards healing the sick, be it through prayer, 'distant-healing' or 'hands-on' healing. Bishop Eric and Br Johanan we have already mentioned, but another person who comes to mind is Sr Hannah, who apart from her duties of Bursar, dedicates a major part of her

Fig. 37. Sr Hannah

spiritual discipline to the healing of both those who are sick and those who are troubled. As already mentioned, Srs Sophia, Mary and Phoebe have all focussed upon healing in their Meditation programmes, which has been central to Order life from the earliest times, (see the notice on page 8).

For the Order, dedicating a life to the well-being of others is not only a means of engaging in the work set by Our Lord, who commanded his disciples thus: "But go rather to the lost sheep of the house of Israel. And as ye go, preach, saying, The kingdom of heaven is at hand. Heal the sick, cleanse the lepers, raise the dead, cast out devils: freely ye have received, freely give" (Matt. 10:6-8), it is also a means of spiritualising that life. In part, this is because the mind is not a vacuum, and if left to its own devices it will inevitably occupy itself with thoughts, feelings and images generated by the senses; a never-ending procession of thought-forms defining and dictating mood and behaviour, and to what purpose? It has long been known that prayer, especially for others, is an effective way of harnessing the same faculties towards more positive and spiritual ends. Consequently, those who dedicate a part of their life to serving others, especially those in need, also engage in the work of *habitus* modification, in short, spiritual transformation.

The daily life of the Order is based upon three offices to be performed daily by individual members. The morning office, ideally performed upon rising, after ablutions, establishes a unique theme and tone for the day. The midday office, a very short office reinforces the primary theme established in the morning office, and the evening office, performed just before retiring, provides time for members to reflect upon personal behaviour and attitudes and to consider possible modifications and responses. These daily offices are primarily designed for individual use but may be shared and used as group devotions. They may also be modified, extended and supplemented with different prayers and readings focussed upon the healing and well-being of others. All of which constitute steps on the Path.

The Path

The 'Path' is a term used to describe the movement from the *habitus* of the first Adam to the second Adam. The path is frequently described as being 'long', 'narrow', 'thorny' and 'difficult' because the change from one *habitus* to another is accepted as being complex and tricky—difficult, but not impossible!

The primitive Church saw the primary work on the Path as changes the catechumen should make in preparation for baptism. These changes were perceived to be on three levels; 1) personal & private; 2) societal & public; 3) spiritual & transcendent. The first is concerned with the attitudes and dispositions of the 'inner' being; the second with our behaviour in society and the third with our relationship with God. All of which could be described as functioning under the first Adam's reactive disposition of 'I like—I don't like'. The objective of the primitive Church was to transform this lower reactive carnal nature of humanity into the higher, selfless spiritual nature; to which the first and second Adam have been applied[1].

The term that best serves the mindset and behavioural reflexes of both is *habitus*, which means those aspects of culture that are expressed in the daily practices of individuals and groups, including, learned habits, bodily skills, styles, tastes, and other non-discursive knowledge. In short, *habitus* represents the way group culture and personal history shapes the body and the mind of the individual, and as a consequence, shapes society. The core focus of the primitive Church was to modify the behavioural reflexes of the First Adam to accommodate a new *habitus* that was conducive to a 'new society.'

This required a new context defined by the teachings of Jesus Christ that are described in the New Testament. The primary focus was threefold: firstly, overcoming selfishness and greed through sharing resources in common; secondly, overcoming anger and aggression through the practice of non-violence; and thirdly, overcoming lust and the desire for vicarious pleasure through acknowledging that the body is the temple of the Holy

---

1   1 Corinthians chapter 15.

Spirit. These three dispositions were fused into a new *habitus* (the Second Adam) through Prayer, Meditation and Fasting.

Essentially there is nothing new in this approach. A tradition of studying the scriptures with this kind of thing in mind had evolved, at least from the Babylonian captivity in the sixth century BC, and possibly long before—each succeeding generation seeking to find meaning in the sacred texts. What was different was the Christian motivation. The primitive Church adopted what had gone before, and carefully mined the scriptures to facilitate the transformation of the *habitus* of the First Adam, and this was employed with great effect, especially in preparing catechumens for baptism; an approach that would often take three or more years to accomplish. In effect, a road-map or guide-book was created that enabled the catechumen to change from one *habitus* to another.

The personal life of the catechumen was spent following this guide, reflecting upon their behaviour in the context of scriptural readings (meditation), and in seeking divine assistance (prayer) to enable them to make the necessary changes. In prayer we commune with God, and in doing so regularly we beat an uncommon path that leads us towards the renewal of our being. A great deal of internal wrestling takes place before our prayer-life is established, wherein the catechumen learns that winning a battle does not mean winning the war. Nevertheless, with persistence victory will be achieved, as history clearly demonstrates.

With this in mind, there follows a compilation of readings that have been used over the centuries as fertile themes for our meditations, thereby assisting aspirants along the path.

St Cyprian

The following compilation is attributed to St Cyprian[2] (d. 258) Bishop of Carthage and Martyr. He was for much of his life a pagan rhetorician before converting to Christianity in c.246. He was consecrated Bp of Carthage, having acquired a profound knowledge of the scriptures, as well as the writings of Tertullian. The following text is from *Ad Quirinum* one of three books addressed to his son.

Cyprian lived in turbulent times; the Decian persecution had began in the autumn of 249, and he was forced to flee, but continued his mission by letter. In 252 the plague broke out in Carthage, for which the Christians were blamed, furthermore, the schism of Novatian emerged, which took up a great deal of Cyprian's time. The Novatian controversy was shortened by the persecution of Christians initiated by the emperor Valerian, during which Cyprian was captured and martyred in Carthage on the 14th of September 258.

Of the benefit of good works and mercy
In Isaiah 58:1-9 "Loose every knot of unrighteousness, let go the choking of impotent engagements. Send away the harassed into rest, and scatter every unrighteous contract. Break your bread to the hungry, and bring the houseless poor into your dwelling. If you see the naked, clothe him; and despise not them of your own seed in your house. Then shall your seasonable light break forth, and your garments shall quickly arise; and righteousness shall go before you: and the glory of God shall surround you. Then you shall cry out, and God shall hear you; while you are yet speaking, He shall say, Here I am."
That charity and brotherly affection are to be steadfastly practised
In Malachi 2:10 "Has not one God created us? Is there not one Father of us all?" of this same thing according to John: "This is my commandment, that you love one another, even as I have loved

---

2 *The Treatises of St Cyprian of Carthage*, Robert E. Wallis, Trans. First Rate Publishers, Wisconsin.

you. Greater love than this has no man, than that one should lay down his life for his friends."

That we must boast in nothing, since nothing is our own

In the Gospel according to John 3:27, "No one can receive anything, except it were given him from heaven." Also in the first Epistle of Paul to the Corinthians 3:7, "For what have you that you have not received? But if you have received it, why do you boast, as if you had not received it?"

That humility and quietness are to be maintained in all things

In Isaiah 66:1, "Thus says the Lord God, The heaven is my throne, and the earth is the stool of my feet. What seat will you build for me, or what is the place for my rest? For all those things has my hand made, and all those things are mine. And upon whom else will I look, except upon the lowly and quiet man, and him that trembles at my words?"

That all good and righteous men suffer more, but ought to endure because they are proved

In Proverbs, 17:3, "The furnace proves the vessels of the potter, and the trial of tribulation righteous men." Also in the fiftieth Psalm, v.17, "The sacrifice to God is a contrite spirit; a contrite and humbled heart God will not despise."

That we must not grieve the Holy Spirit, whom we have received

Paul the apostle to the Ephesians 4:30, "Grieve not the Holy Spirit of God, in which you were sealed in the day of redemption. Let all bitterness, and wrath, and indignation, and clamour, and blasphemy be taken away from you."

That anger must be overcome

In Proverbs 16:32, "Better is a patient man than a strong man; for he who restrains his anger is better than he who takes a city." Also in the same place: "The imprudent man declares his anger on the same day, but the crafty man hides away his dishonour." Of this same thing to the Ephesians 4:26, "Be angry, and sin not. Let not the sun set upon your wrath."

That brethren ought to support one another

To the Galatians 6:1, "Each one having others in consideration lest you also should be tempted. Bear one another's burdens, and so you shall fulfil the law of Christ."

That we must trust in God only, and in Him we must glory

In Jeremiah 9:23, "Let not the wise man glory in his wisdom, neither let the strong man glory in his strength, nor let the rich man glory in his riches; but let him that glories glory in this, that he understands and knows that I am the Lord, who does mercy, and judgment, and righteousness upon the earth, because in them is my pleasure, says the Lord."

That he who has attained to trust, having put off the former man, ought to regard only celestial and spiritual things, and to give no heed to the world which he has already renounced

In Isaiah 55:6, "Seek the Lord; and when you have found Him, call upon Him. But when he has come near unto you, let the wicked forsake his ways, and the unrighteous man his thoughts; and let him be turned unto the Lord, and he shall obtain mercy, because He will plentifully pardon your sins."

That we must not swear (an oath)

In Ecclesiasticus 23:11, "A man that swears much shall be filled with iniquity, and the plague shall not depart from his house; and if he swear vainly' he shall not be justified." Of this same matter, according to Matthew 5:34, "Again you have heard that it was said to them of old, you shall not swear falsely, but shall perform unto the Lord your oaths. I say unto you, Swear not at all: neither by heaven, because it is God's throne, nor by the earth, because it is His footstool; nor by Jerusalem, because it is the city of the great king; neither shall you swear by your head, because you can not make one hair white or black. But let your discourse be, Yea, yea; Nay, nay: (for whatever is fuller than these is of evil.")

That you must not curse

In Exodus 8:28, "You shall not curse nor speak ill of the ruler of your people." Also, in the thirty-third Psalm: "Restrain your tongue from evil, and your lips that they speak no guile." Of the same matter, according to Matthew 12:36, "But I say unto you. That every idle word which men shall speak, they shall give account of it in the day of judgement. For by your words you shall be justified, and by your words you shall be condemned."

That we must never murmur, but bless God concerning all things that happen

In Job 2:10, "If we have received good things from the Lord's hand, why shall we not endure evil things? In all these things which happened unto him, Job sinned not with his lips in the sight of the Lord."

That men are tried by God for this purpose, that they may be proved.

In Deuteronomy 13:3, "The Lord your God proves you, that he may know you love the Lord your God with all of your heart and all of your soul." Of the same thing in the Wisdom of Solomon 3:4, "Although in the sight of men they suffered torments, their hope is full of immortality; and having been in few things distressed, yet in many things they shall be happily ordered, because God tried them, and found them worthy of Himself. As gold in the furnace He proved them, and as a burnt-offering He received them."

Of the benefits of martyrdom

According to Luke 6:22, blessed shall you be when men shall hate you, and shall separate you, and shall drive you out, and shall speak evil of your name, as wicked, for the son of man's sake. Rejoice in that day, and exult, for, lo, your reward is great in heaven."

There is nothing to be preferred to the love of God & Christ

In the Gospel according to Matthew 10:37, "He that loves father or mother above me, is not worthy of me; and he that loves son or daughter above me is not worthy of me; and he that takes not up his cross and follows me, is not my disciple."

That we are not to obey our own will, but the will of God

In the gospel according to John 6:38, "I came not down from heaven to do my own will, but the will of Him that sent me." In the Gospel according to Matthew 26:39, "Father, if it be possible, let this cup pass from me; nevertheless, not what I will, but what you will."

That the foundation and strength of hope and faith is fear
In the 110th Psalm: "The fear of the Lord is the beginning of wisdom." In the Wisdom of Solomon, and Proverbs 9:10, "The beginning of wisdom is to fear God."

That we must not rashly judge one another
In the gospel of Luke 6:37, "Judge not, that you be not judged; condemn not, that you be not condemned." In Romans 14:4, "Who are you that judge another man's servant? To his own master he stands or falls."

That when we have received a wrong, we must remit and forgive it
In the Lord's Prayer: "Forgive us our debts, even as we forgive our debtors." Also according to Mark 11:25, "And when you stand for prayer, forgive, if you have ought against anyone, that also your Father who is in heaven may forgive you your sins. But if you do not forgive, neither will your Father which is in heaven forgive you your sins." Also in the same place: "In what measure you mete, in that shall it be measured to you again."

That evil is not to be returned for evil
In the Epistle of Paul to the Romans 12:17-21, "Rendering to no man evil for evil." Also, in Revelations 22:11-12, "And he said unto me, seal not the words of the prophecy of this book: because now the time is at hand. And let those who persist in hunting, hunt; and let him who is filthy, be filthy still: but let the righteous do still more righteousness: and in like manner, let him that is holy do still more holiness. Behold, I come quickly; and my reward is with me, to render every man according to his deeds."

That it is impossible to attain to the Father but by His Son Jesus Christ
In the Gospel according to John 14:6, "I am the way, the truth and the life; no man comes unto the Father, but by me." Also in the same place: "I am the door: by me if any man enter in, he shall be saved."

That unless a man have been baptized and born again, he cannot attain unto the kingdom of God

In the Gospel according to John 3:5, "Unless a man be born again of water and the Spirit, he cannot enter into the kingdom of God. For that which is born of the flesh is flesh; and that which is born of the Spirit is spirit

That it is of small account to be baptized and to receive the Eucharist, unless one profit by it both in deed and works

In the Gospel according to Matthew 3:10, "Every tree that brings not forth good fruit shall be cut down, and cast into the fire." Also in the same place (Matt 7:22); "Many shall say unto me in that day, Lord, Lord, have we not prophesied in Your name, and in Your name have cast out devils, and in Your name done great works? And then shall I say to them, I never knew you; depart from me, you who work iniquity."

That even a baptized person loses the grace he has attained unless he keeps himself innocent

In the Gospel according to John 5:14, "Lo, you are made whole: sin no more, lest a worse thing happen to you." Also, in the first epistle of Paul to the Corinthians 3:16, "Do you not know that you are the temple of God, and the Spirit of God abides in you? If any one violate the temple of God him will God destroy." Also in the second book of Chronicles 15:2, "God is with you, while you are with Him; If you forsake Him, He will forsake you."

That remission cannot in the Church be granted unto him who has sinned against the Holy Ghost

In the Gospel according to Matthew 12:32, "Whosoever shall say a word against the Son of man, it shall be forgiven him; but whosoever shall speak against the Holy Ghost it shall not be forgiven him, neither in this world, nor in the world to come." Also according to Mark 3: 28-30, "All sins shall be forgiven, and blasphemies, to the sons of men; but whoever shall blaspheme against the Holy Ghost, it shall not be forgiven him."

That it was before predicted, concerning the hatred of the name
In the Gospel according to Matthew 10:22, "And you shall be hated of all men for my name's sake." Also according to John 15:18, "If the world hates you, know that it first hated me. If you were of the world, the world would love what would be its own: but because you are not of the world. And I have chosen you out of the world, therefore the world hates you. Remember the word which I said unto you, the servant is not greater than his lord. If they have persecuted me, they will also persecute you."

That what any one has vowed to God, he must repay quickly
In Ecclesiastes 5:4, "According as you have vowed a vow to God, delay not to pay it." Of this same matter in the forty-ninth Psalm: "Sacrifice to God the sacrifice of praise, and pay your vows to the most high, call upon me in the day of trouble, I will deliver you, and you shall glorify me."

That he who does not believe is judged already
In the Gospel according to John 3:18, "He that believes not is already judged, because he has not believed in the name of the only Son of God. And this is the judgement, that light has come into the world, and men have loved darkness rather than light."

Of the benefit of virginity and continence
In the Gospel according to Matthew 19:11, "All men do not receive the word, but they to whom it is given: for there are some eunuchs who were born so from their mothers womb, and there are eunuchs who have been constrained by men, and there are eunuchs who have made themselves eunuchs for the kingdom of heaven's sake. He who can receive it, let him receive it."

That the Father judges nothing, but the Son; and that the Father is not glorified by him by whom the Son is not glorified
In the gospel according to John 5:22, "The Father judges nothing, but has given all judgement unto the Son, that all may honour the Son as they honour the Father. He who honours not the Son, honours not the Father who has sent Him."

That the believer ought not to live like the Gentile
In Jeremiah 10:2, "Thus says the Lord, walk not according to the way of the Gentiles." Also, in Isaiah: "Go forth from the midst of them, you who bear the vessels of the Lord."

That God is patient for this end, that we may repent of our sins, and be reformed
In Romans 2:4-6, "Do you despise the riches of His goodness, and forbearance, and patience, not knowing that the goodness of God leads you to repentance? But according to your hardness and impenitent heart, you store up to yourself wrath in the day of wrath and of revelation of the just judgment of God, who will render to every man according to his deeds."

That the believer ought not to be punished for other offences, except for the name he bears
In the first Epistle of Peter 4:15, "Nor let any of you suffer as a thief, or a murderer, or as an evil-doer, or as a minder of other people's business, but as a Christian.

That the servant of God ought to be innocent, lest he falls into secular punishment.
In the Epistle of Paul to the Romans 13:3, "Will you not be afraid of the powers, do that which is good, and you shall have praise of it."

That there is given to us an example of living in Christ
In the first Epistle of Peter 2:21, "For Christ suffered for us, leaving you an example that you may follow His steps; who did no sin, neither was guile found in His mouth; who, when he was reviled, reviled not again; when he suffered, threatened not, but gave Himself up to him that judges unrighteously." Also, Paul to the Philippians: "Who, being appointed in the figure of God, thought it not robbery that He was equal with God; but emptied Himself, taking the form of a servant, He was made in the likeness of man, and was found in fashion as a man. He humbled Himself, becoming obedient even unto death, and the death of the cross. For which cause also God has exalted Him, and has given Him a name, that which may be above every name, that in the name of Jesus every knee should be bowed, of things

heavenly, and earthly, and infernal; and that every tongue should confess that the Lord Jesus Christ is in glory of God the Father." Of this same thing in the Gospel according to John: "If I have washed your feet, being your Master and Lord, you also ought to wash the feet of others. For I have given you an example that as I have done, you also should do to others."

That we must not labour noisily nor boastfully

In the Gospel according to Matthew 6:3, "Let not your left hand know what your right hand does, that your alms may be in secret; and your Father, which sees in secret, shall render to you."

That we must not speak foolishly and offensively

In Paul's Epistle to the Ephesians 5:4, "Foolish speaking and scurrility, which are not fitting for the occasion, let them not be even named among you."

That faith is of advantage altogether, and that we can do as much as we believe

In Isaiah 7:9, "And if you do not believe, neither shall you understand." Also, in the gospel according to Matthew 17:20, "If you have faith as a grain of mustard seed, you shall say to this mountain, pass over from here to that place, and it shall pass over; and nothing shall be impossible unto you." Also according to Mark 11:24, "All things whatsoever you pray and ask for, believe that you shall receive them, and they shall be yours."

That hope is of future things, and therefore that our faith concerning those things which are promised ought to be patient

In the Epistle of Paul to the Romans 8:24, "We are saved by hope. But hope that is seen is not hope; for what a man sees, why does he hope for? But if we hope for what we see not, we hope for it in patience."

That it arises from our fault and our desert that we suffer, and do not perceive God's help in everything

In Hosea 4:1, "Hear the word of the Lord, you children of Israel: because judgment is from the Lord against the inhabitants of the earth because there is neither mercy nor truth, nor acknowledgment of God upon the earth; but cursing, and lying, and slaughter, and theft, and adultery is scattered abroad upon the earth: they mingle blood to blood. Therefore the land shall mourn, with all its inhabitants, with the beasts of the field, with the creeping things of the earth, with the birds of heaven; and the fishes of the sea shall fail."

That we must not take usury

In the thirteenth Psalm: "He that has not given his money upon usury, and has not received gifts concerning the innocent. He who does these things shall not be moved for ever." Also in Ezekiel 22:30, "But the man who will be righteous, shall not oppress a man, and shall return the pledge of the debtor, and shall not commit rapine, and shall give his bread to the hungry, and shall cover the naked, and shall not give his money for usury." Also in Deuteronomy 23:19, "You shall not lend to your brother with usury of money, and with usury of victuals."

That even our enemies must be loved

In the Gospel according to Luke 6:32, "If you love those who love you, what reward do you have? For even sinners love those who love them." Also according to Matthew 5:44, "Love your enemies, and pray for those who persecute you, that you may be the children of your Father who is in heaven, who makes His sun to rise upon the good and the evil, and gives rain upon the righteous and the unrighteous."

That the sacrament of faith must not be profaned

In Proverbs 23:9, "Say not anything in the ears of a foolish man; lest, when he hears it, he may mock your wise words." Also in the Gospel according to Matthew 7:6, "Give not that which is holy to dogs; neither cast your pearls before the swine, lest perchance they trample them down with their feet, and turn again and crush you."

That no one should be uplifted in his labour

In the Gospel according to Luke 17: 7-10, "Which of you, having a servant ploughing, or a shepherd, says to him when he comes from the field, pass forward and recline? But says to him, make ready somewhat that I may sup, and gird yourself, and minister to me, until I eat and drink; and afterwards you shall eat and drink? Does he thank that servant because he had done that which is commanded?"

That the liberty of believing or not believing is placed in free choice

In Deuteronomy 30:15, "Lo, I have set before your face life and death, good and evil. Choose for yourself life that you may live." Also in Isaiah 1:19, "And if you be willing, and hear me, you shall eat the good of the land. But if you be unwilling, and will not hear me, the sword shall consume you. For the mouth of the Lord has spoken these things."

That the secrets of God cannot be seen through, and therefore that our faith ought to be simple

In the first Epistle of Paul to the Corinthians 13:12, "We see now through the glass in an enigma, but then with face to face. Now I know partly; but then shall I know even as also I am known." Also in the Wisdom of Solomon 1:1, "And in simplicity of heart seek Him." Also in Philippians 2:4, "Seek not things higher than yourself," Also in Ecclesiastes 7:16, "Be not excessively righteous, and do not reason more than is required."

That no one is without filth and without sin

In Job 14:4, "For who is pure from filth? No one; even if his life be of one day on the earth." Also in the first Epistle of John 1:18, "If we say that we have no sin, we deceive ourselves, and the truth is not in us."

That we must not please men, but God

In the fifty-second Psalm: "They that please men are confounded, because God has made them nothing." Also in the Epistle of Paul to the Galatians 1:10, "If I wished to please men I should not be the servant of Christ."

That nothing that is done is hidden from God

In Proverbs 15:3, "In every place the eyes of God look upon the good and evil." Also in the first book of Samuel 16:7, "Man looks on the face, but God on the heart."

That the believer is amended and reserved

In the one hundred and seventeenth Psalm: "The Lord amending has amended me, and has not delivered me to death." Also in Malachi 3:3, "And He shall sit melting and purifying, as it were, gold and silver; and He shall purify the sons of Levi."

That no one should be made sad by death; since in living is labour and peril, in dying peace and the certainty of resurrection

In the first Epistle to Corinthians 15:36, "You fool, that which you sow is not quickened except it have first died." And again: "Star differs from star in glory: so also the resurrection. The body is sown in corruption, it rises without corruption; it is sown in ignominy, it rises again in glory, it is sown in weakness, it rises again in power; it is sown an animal body, it rises again a spiritual body."

Of the idols which the Gentiles think to be gods

In the Wisdom of Solomon: 15:15, "All the idols of the nations they counted gods, which neither have the use of their eyes for seeing, nor their nostrils to receive breath, nor their ears for hearing, nor the fingers on their hands for handling; but their feet also are slow to walk. For man made them; and he who has borrowed his breath, he fashioned them."

That too great a lust for food is not to be desired

The Epistle to the Romans 14:17, "The kingdom of God is not meat and drink, but righteousness, and peace, and joy in the Holy Ghost." In the Gospel according to John 4:32, "I have meat which you know not of. My meat is that I should do His will who sent me, and should finish His work."

That the lust of possessing, and money, are not to be sought for

In the gospel according to Mark 8:36, For what does it profit a man to make a gain of the whole world, but that he should lose himself?" In the first Epistle to Timothy 6:7, "We brought nothing into this world, but neither can we take anything away. Therefore, having maintenance and clothing let us with these be content." And again: "For the root of all evils is covetousness, which some, coveting, have made shipwreck from the faith, and have plunged themselves in many sorrows."

That the sin of fornication is grievous

In the first Epistle of Paul to the Corinthians 6:18, "Every sin whatsoever a man does is outside the body; but he who commits fornication sins against his own body. You are not your own, for you are bought with a great price. Glorify and bear the Lord in your body."

What are those carnal things which beget death, and what are the spiritual things which lead to life

Paul to the Galatians 5:7, "The flesh lusts against the Spirit, and the Spirit against the flesh: for they are contrary the one to the other, that you cannot do even those things which you wish. But the deeds of the flesh are manifest, which are: adulteries, fornications, impurities, filthiness, idolatries, sorceries, murders, hatreds, strife, emulations, animosities, provocations, dissensions, heresies, envying, drunkenness, revelling, and such like; With respect to which I declare, that they who do such things shall not possess the kingdom of God. But the fruit of the Spirit is charity, joy, peace, magnanimity, goodness, faith, gentleness, continence, chastity. For they who are Christ's have crucified their flesh, with its vices and lusts.

That all sins are put away in Baptism

In the first Epistle of Paul to the Corinthians 6:9, "Neither fornicators, nor those who serve idols, nor adulterers, nor the effeminate, nor the lusters after mankind, nor thieves, nor cheaters, nor drunkards, nor revilers, nor robbers, shall attain the kingdom of God. And these things indeed you were: but you are washed, but you are sanctified in the name of the Lord Jesus Christ, and in the Spirit of our God."

That the discipline of God is to be observed in the Church Precepts

In Jeremiah 3:15, "And I will give to you shepherds according to my own heart; and they shall feed the sheep, feeding them with discipline." Also in the Proverbs 3:11, "My son neglect not the discipline of God, nor fail when rebuked by Him. For whom God loves, He rebukes."

For it was foretold that men should despise sound discipline

Paul in the second Epistle to Timothy 4:3, "There will be a time when they shall not endure sound doctrine; but according to their own lusts will heap to themselves teachers itching in hearing, tickling their ears; and shall turn away their hearing indeed from the truth, but they shall converted unto fables."

That we must depart from him who lives irregularly and contrary to discipline

Paul to the Thessalonians 3:6, "But we have commanded you, in the name of Jesus Christ, that you depart from all brethren who walk disorderly, and not according to the tradition which they have received from us."

That the kingdom of God is not in the wisdom of the world, nor in eloquence, but in the faith of the cross, and in virtue of conversation.

In the first Epistle of Paul to the Corinthians 1:17, "Christ sent me to preach, not in wisdom of discourse, lest the cross of Christ should become of no effect. For the word of the cross is foolishness to those who perish; but to those who are saved it is the power of God. For it is written, I will destroy the wisdom of the wise, and I will reprove the prudence of the prudent. Where is the wise? Where is the scribe? Where is the disputer of this world? Hath not God made foolish the wisdom of this world. Since indeed, in the wisdom of God, the world by wisdom knew not God, it pleased God by the foolishness of preaching to save them that believe. Because the Jews desire signs and the Greeks seek for wisdom: but we preach Christ crucified, to the Jews indeed a stumbling block, and to the Gentiles foolishness; but to them that are called, Jews and Greeks, Christ the power of God, and the wisdom of God."

That we must obey parents

In the Epistle of Paul to the Ephesians 6:1, "Children, be obedient to your parents: for this is right. Honour your father and your mother that it may be well with you, and you may be long-lived on the earth."

And that fathers also should not be harsh in respect of their children

Also in the same place (Eph. 6:4), "And, you fathers drive not your children to wrath: but nourish them in the discipline and rebuke of the Lord."

That servants, when they have believed, ought to serve their carnal masters the better
In the Epistle of Paul to the Ephesians 6:5, "Servants, obey you fleshly masters with fear and trembling, and all simplicity of your heart, as to Christ; not serving for the eye, as if you were pleasing men, but as servants of God.

Moreover, the masters should be more gentle
Also in the same place (Eph. 6:9), "And you masters, do the same things to them, forbearing anger; knowing that both your Master and theirs is in heaven; and there is no choice of persons with Him."

That every person ought to have care rather of his own people, and especially of believers
The apostle in his first Epistle to Timothy 5:8, "But if any take not care of his own, and especially of those of his own household, he denies the faith, and is worse than an infidel." Of the same thing in Isaiah 58:7, "If you see the naked, clothe him; and despise not those who are of the household of your own seed."

That an elder must not be rashly accused
In the first to Timothy 5:19, "Against an elder receive not all accusation."

That the sinner must be publicly reproved
In the first Epistle of Paul to Timothy 5:20, "Rebuke them that sin in the presence of all, that others also may be afraid."

That we must not speak with heretics
In Titus 3:10, "A man that is a heretic, after one rebuke avoid; knowing that one of such sort is perverted, and sins, and is by his own self condemned. Also, in the second Epistle to Timothy 2:17, "Their word does creep as a canker."

That innocency asks with confidence, and obtains
In the first Epistle of John 3:20, "If our heart blame us not, we have confidence towards God; and whatever we ask, we shall receive from Him." Also in the gospel according to Matthew 5: 8, "Blessed are they of a pure heart, for they shall see God." Also

in the twenty-third Psalm: "Who shall ascend into the hill of the Lord? Or who shall stand in His holy place? The innocent in hands and of a pure heart."

That the devil has no power against man unless God have allowed it

In the gospel according to John 19:11, "Jesus said, you could have no power against me, unless it were given you from above." Also in Job, first of all God permitted, and then it was allowed to the devil."

That the wages be quickly paid to the hireling

In Leviticus 19:13, "The wages of your hireling shall not sleep with you until the morning."

That divination must not be used

In Deuteronomy 18:10-12: "Do not use omens or auguries."

That a schism must not be made, even though he who withdraws should remain in one faith

In the 132nd Psalm: "Behold how good and how pleasant a thing it is that brethren should dwell in unity!" And in the gospel according to Matthew 12:30, "He that is not with me is against me; and he that gather not with me, scatters." Also, in the first Epistle of Paul to the Corinthians 1:10-17, "But I beseech you, brethren, by the name of the Lord Jesus Christ, that you all say the same thing, and that there be no schisms among you; but that you be all joined together in the same mind and in the same opinion."

That believers ought to be simple, with prudence

In the gospel according to Matthew 10:16, "Be as prudent as serpents, and simple as doves."

That a brother must not be deceived

In the first Epistle of Paul to the Thessalonians 4:6, "That a man does not deceive his brother in a matter, because God is the avenger for all these."

That the end of the world comes suddenly

In the first Epistle to the Thessalonians 5:2, "the day of the Lord shall come as a thief in the night. When they shall say, Peace and Security, then on them shall come sudden destruction." Also in the Acts of the Apostles 1:7, No one can know the times or the seasons which the Father has placed in His own power."

That every one is tempted so much as he is able to bear
In the first Epistle of Paul to the Corinthians 10:13, "No temptation shall take you, except such is human. But God is faithful, who will not suffer you to be tempted above what you are able; but will with the temptation also make a way to escape, that you may be able to bear it."

That not everything is to be done which is lawful
Paul, in the first Epistle to the Corinthians 10:23, "all things are lawful, but all things are not expedient: all things are lawful, but all things edify not."

That it was foretold that heresies would arise
In the first Epistle of Paul to the Corinthians 11:19, "Heresies must need be, in order that they which are approved may be made manifest among you."

That the Eucharist is to be received with fear and honour
In Leviticus: "But whatever soul shall eat of the flesh of the sacrifice of salvation, which is the Lord's, and his uncleanness is still upon him, that soul shall perish from his people." Also in the first to Corinthians 11:27, "Whosoever shall eat the bread or drink the cup of the Lord unworthily shall be guilty of the body and blood of the Lord."

That we are to live with the good, but to avoid the evil
In the first Epistle of Paul to the Corinthians 15:33, "Evil communications corrupt good dispositions."

That we must labour not with word, but with deeds
In Paul, the first Epistle to the Corinthians 4:20, "The kingdom of God is not in word, but in power." In the gospel according to Matthew 7:4, "Every one who hears my words, and does them I will liken him to a wise man who built his house upon rock. The rain descended, the floods came, the winds blew, and beat upon the house, and it fell not."

That judgement will be according to the times, either of equity before the law, or of law after Moses
Paul to the Romans 2:12, "As many as have sinned without law, shall perish without law; and as many have sinned in the law, shall be judged also by the law."

That the grace of God ought to be without price
In the Acts of the Apostles 8:20, "Your money be in perdition with yourself, because you have thought that the grace of God is possessed by money. And in the Gospel according to Matthew 10:8, "Freely you have received, freely give."

That the Holy Spirit has frequently appeared as fire
In Exodus 19:18, "And the whole of Mount Sinai smoked, because God had come down upon it in fire." Also in the Acts of the Apostles 2:2, "And suddenly there was made a sound from heaven, as if a vehement blast were borne along, and it filled the whole of that place in which they were sitting. And there appeared to them cloven tongues as if of fire, which also settled upon each of them; and they were all filled with the Holy Ghost." Also in the sacrifices, whatsoever God accounted acceptable, fire descended from heaven, which consumed what was sacrificed.

That all good men ought willingly to hear rebuke
In Proverbs 9:7, He who reproves a wicked man shall be hated by him. Rebuke a wise man, and he will love you."

That we must abstain from much speaking
In Proverbs 10:19, "Out of much speaking you shall not escape sin; but sparing your lips, you shall be wise.

That we must not lie
In Proverbs 12:22, "Lying lips are an abomination to the Lord."

That they are frequently to be corrected who do wrong in domestic duty
In Proverbs 13:24, "He who spares the rod, hates his son." And again: "Do not cease from correcting the child."

That when a wrong is received, patience is to be maintained, and vengeance to be left to God.
In Romans 12:19, Dearly beloved, avenge not yourselves, but rather give place unto wrath; for it is written, vengeance is mine; I will repay, says the Lord."

That we must not use detraction
In Proverbs 24:17, Do not rejoice when your enemy falls, And do not let your heart be glad when he stumbles;" Also in Titus 3:2, "To speak evil of no man."

That we must not lay snares against our neighbour
In Proverbs 26:27, "He who digs a pit for his neighbour, himself shall fall into it."
The sick are to be visited
In Ecclesiasticus 7:35, "Be not slack to visit the sick man; for from these things you shall be strengthened in love."
The tale-bearers are accursed
In Proverbs 18:8, "The words of a gossip are like wounds; they go down to the innermost parts of the belly.
That the sacrifices of the wicked are not acceptable
In Ecclesiasticus 34:19, "The Highest approves not the gifts of the unrighteous."
That those are more severely judged, who in this world have had more power
James 3:1, The hardest judgement shall be made on those who govern."
That the widow and orphans ought to be protected
In Sirach 4:10, "Be merciful to the orphans as a father, and as a husband to their mother, and you shall be the son of the Highest." Also in Exodus 22:22, "You shall not afflict any widow and orphan. But if you afflict them, and they cry out and call unto me, I will hear their crying, and will be angry in mind against you: and I will destroy you with the sword, and your wives will be widows and your children orphans."
That one ought to make confession while he is in the flesh
In the fifth Psalm: "But in the grave who will confess unto you?" Also in the twenty-ninth Psalm: "Shall the dust make confession unto you?"
That flattery is pernicious
In Isaiah, 3:9, "They who call you blessed, lead you into error, and trouble the paths of your feet."
That God is more loved by him who has had many sins forgiven in baptism
In the Gospel according to Luke 7:47: "To whom much is forgiven, he loves much; and to whom little is forgiven, the same loves little."

That there is a strong conflict to be waged against the devil, and that therefore we ought to stand bravely, that we may be able to conquer

In the Epistle of Paul to the Ephesians 6:12, "Our wrestle is not against flesh and blood, but against the powers and princes of this world, and of the darkness; against the spiritual things of wickedness in the heavenly places." Also in the same place; "Because of this put on the whole armour of God, that you may be able to resist in the most evil day; that when you have accomplished all, you may stand, having your loins girt in the truth of the Gospel, putting on the breastplate of righteousness, and having your feet shod with the preparation of the Gospel of Peace; In all things taking the shield of faith in which you may extinguish all the fiery darts of the most wicked one; and take the helmet of salvation, and the sword of the Spirit, which is the word of God."

Also of Antichrist, that he will come as a man

In Isaiah, 14:17, "This is the man who arouses the earth, who disturbs kings, who makes the whole earth a desert."

That the yoke of the law was heavy, which is cast off by us, and that the Lord's yoke is easy, which is taken up by us

In the Gospel according to Matthew 11:28-29, "Come unto me, you who labour and are burdened, and I will make you to rest. Take my yoke upon you; and learn of me: for I am meek and lowly of heart, and you shall find rest for your souls. For my yoke is good, and my burden is light."

That we are to be urgent in our prayers

In the Epistle of Paul to the Colossians 4:2-4, "Be instant in prayer, and watch therein." Also in the first Psalm: "But in the law of the Lord is his will, and in His law will he meditate day and night."

Bibliography & Early References

For a general bibliography, and more extensive references and discussions concerning the Church in Roman and post-Roman Britain see:

Anson, Peter F. *Bishops at Large,* (London, Faber & Faber, 1964)

Bede, *The Ecclesiastical History of the English Nation,* (London, Everymans Library, J.M. Dent & Sons.)

Boon, G.C. *Traces of Romano-British Christianity in the West Country,* (see the *Transactions* of the Bristol & Gloucestershire Archaeological Society, Vol. 110, pp. 37-52, 1992)

Browne, G.F. *The Christian Church in These Islands Before the Coming of Augustine.* (London, SPCK, New York, The Macmillan Co. 1923)

Br. Matthias *Notes, Prayers, Services & Readings of the Liturgical Year* (Bristol, ODP Publications, 2017)

Budge, E.A. Wallis, *The Paradise of the Holy Fathers,* (London, Chatto & Windus, 1907)

Collier, Jeremy, *An Ecclesiastical History of Great Britain* (London, William Straker, 1852)

Engen, John Van (trans.) *Devotio Moderna, Basic Writings,* (New York, Paulist Press, 1988)

Ferrar, W. J. trans: *The Proof of the Gospel* (Grand Rapids, Michigan, Baker Book House Co., 1981)

Haddan, A & Stubbs, W: *Councils and Ecclesiastical Documents Relating to Great Britain & Ireland,* Oxford, Clarendon Press, 1869)

Hall, Stuart George (trans.), *Gregory of Nyssa, Homilies on the Beatitudes,* (Brill, Leiden 2000)

Kreider, Alan, *The Patient Ferment of the Early Church* (Grand Rapids, Baker Academic, 2016)

Lienhard, Joseph T. (trans.) *Homilies on Luke*, (The Fathers of the Church Vol 94, Catholic University of America Press, 1996)

Mawer, Frances, *Evidence for Christianity in Roman Britain, The Small Finds*, (British Archaeological Reports 243, Oxford 1995)

Petts, David, *Christianity in Roman Britain*, (Stroud, Tempus Publishing Ltd. 2003)

A Roberts & J. Donaldson, (Ed.) *The Ante-Nicene Fathers* (Wm. B. Eerdmans Pub. Co. Grand Rapids, Michigan, 1963)

Scheck, Thomas, (trans.) *Origen: Homilies 1 - 14 on Ezekiel* (The Newman Press, New York, 2010)

Spenser, John & Anne, *Spirit Within Her* (London, Boxtree Ltd. 1994)

Thomas, Charles, *Christianity in Roman Britain to AD 500.* (London, Batsford Academic and Educational Ltd. 1981)

Thompson, E.A. *Saint Germanus of Auxerre and the End of Roman Britain*, (Suffolk, The Boydell Press, 1984)

Ussher, James, *A Discourse on the Religion Anciently Professed by the Irish and British*, (Dublin, John Jones 1815)

Williams, Hugh, *Christianity in Early Britain*, (Oxford, 1912)

———————— *Gildas De Excidio Brittanniae*, (Lampeter, Llanerch Press, Cribyn, facsimile edition, 2006)

Appendix 1

Background Information

The Holy Celtic Church is one of several small churches that emerged in the post second World War period of the 20th century. Arguably, this flowering of autocephalous Churches, which began after World War I, was due in part to public dissatisfaction with the changing role and attitudes of the major churches, and in part inspired by the perceived spiritual idealism of the primitive British Churches. This ancient Church, more commonly thought of today as the Celtic Church, is widely believed to have been established in Roman Britain long before Augustine's mission in 597 AD, although opinions differ concerning when this actually took place. Some historians argue that the Church was established in the second or third century, whilst others believe the Church was first planted in Britain in the middle of the First Century. Whatever the truth might be concerning this question, and in all probability we will never know for certain, it is reasonably clear from archaeological evidence[1] that Christianity was established in Roman Britain for a very long time before Augustine arrived.

The ancient British Church consisted of Christian communities sharing the same beliefs and rites, yet working autonomously under the jurisdiction of independent bishops. However, following the Fourth Century reforms of Constantine and his successors, fundamental differences arose between the Celtic Church and the increasingly powerful Church of Rome over jurisdiction and the keeping of Easter. These differences are nowhere better exemplified than in the long-running conflict between the increasingly dominant orthodoxy of Augustine of Hippo and the radical thinking of the British monk Pelagius. As the political influence and power of the Roman Church grew so the the influence of the British Church declined, a long and slow decline that involved several factors, one of which was a long period of civil conflict.

---

1   See Petts, David, *Christianity in Roman Britain to AD 500*. (London Batsford Academic and Educational Ltd. 1981)

Gildas, a Briton and a monk who lived in the first half of the sixth century, relates in his work *De Excidio Brittaniae* (the oldest surviving record of post-Roman Britain), that following the withdrawal of the Roman legions in the late fourth century, Britain was left without appropriate military defences, and became subject to frequent predatory attacks and raids from the Picts in the North, who raided on land across the northern border and by sea along the East Coast, and from Irish raiders in the West. At the same time internal civil conflicts that frequently turned into civil war, tore apart the fabric of Romano-British society, resulting in a state of social anarchy which prevailed for much of the time throughout the fifth and sixth centuries. This situation was further exacerbated by Anglo-Saxon invaders who from the mid-fifth century onwards accelerated their territorial expansion, and whose depredations upon the indigenous population destabilised the British Church to such an extent that the Chuch and many of its clergy were driven from eastern and central Britain into the West of Britain, the Highlands of both Scotland and Wales and across the sea to Ireland. Many fled to the region of Gaul we now know as Brittany.

Monasticism reached Britain in the fifth century. Monastic settlements such as Bardsey Island and Llangdfan, which were established by St. Cadfan in the fifth century, were often located in isolated areas of western and northern Britain. However, Ireland, being generally free from the turmoil of the mainland, proved to be a more conducive environment for monastic communities. It was probably around such settlements that the ancient Church rallied, consolidated its resources and began to rebuild itself. It is likely that Patrick's mission in Ireland started from such communities. Be that as it may, in 597 AD, Augustine began his mission of persuading the much reduced British Church to accept the authority of Rome, and converting the Anglo-Saxons to Roman Christianity. At first the British Church resisted Augustine's overtures, but eventually, at the Synod of Whitby 664 AD, many of the bishops were persuaded to accept Roman authority, thus the ancient British and new Anglo-Saxon jurisdictions were fused into one. Over the course of time most of the ancient church was slowly absorbed into the Church of Rome.

During the Reformation, and after the accession of Elizabeth I, Roman Catholicism, including whatever remained of the ancient British Church, was proscribed and persecuted by law, which effectively brought about the extinction of the ancient Church. And so it remained until the nineteenth century, when for various reasons, one of which was a Celtic renaissance, a considerable number of committed Christians were inspired to pursue the ideal of the simple and pure spirituality that they perceived in the primitive British Church. Their vision was initially realised when an independent canonical jurisdiction was established in Britain by Jules Ferrette, who had been consecrated on June 2nd 1866, as Mar Julius of Iona, by Peter III, the Syrian Orthodox Patriarch of Antioch and the East. He commissioned Mar Julius as Patriarchal Legate for Western Europe with the power to erect there an indigenous autocephalous patriarchate. The hierarchy was thus restored in the person of Julius of Iona.

The succession continued with the Rev Richard Williams Morgan, whom Mar Julius consecrated in 1874, as Mar Pelagius I, Hierarch of Caerleon-on-Usk. However, British autocephalous churches were not consolidated until bishops of the Old Catholic Church – which rejected Papal supremacy – were established in Britain with the consecration in 1908 of the Rev Arnold Harris Mathew. The lines of succession transmitted by Ferrette and Mathew were eventually conferred in 1944, upon the person of the Rev H.G. De Willmott-Newman, who as Mar Georgius, took on the role of Metropolitan of Glastonbury. Through Mar Georgius' work in furthering the restoration of the ancient Church, a number of autocephalous bodies dedicated to this end, have come into being - among them the Holy Celtic Church.

The Holy Celtic Church is a Sacramental and Trinitarian Christian Church whose beliefs are enshrined in both the Apostles' Creed and the Nicene Creed. It adheres to the *Glastonbury Rite 1984,* (a version of Mar Georgius' Glastonbury Rite revised by Mar Francis), and recommends the *New King*

James Bible for general use. The mission of the Church is to assist people in the spiritual life, following the commendation of the Lord, "*Seek first the kingdom of God*"[2], and is therefore committed to developing the interior life of the soul, with the principal emphasis being upon instructing spiritually motivated people in the devotional work of prayer and meditation, and ancillary spiritual disciplines that further the contemplative life; and to foster a greater understanding and tolerance between the people of this world. To this end the clergy of the Church, all of whom live and work in the community without stipend, have dedicated their lives.

Based in the West Country the membership of the Holy Celtic Church is few in number and spread throughout the region. It consists of small communities that function under the guidance of their local HCC priests, meeting for worship, group devotions and community matters in private oratories and chapels. The current primate is Bishop Marcus, who succeeded Bishop Francis in 1991. The governance of the Church is administered by a Committee of Synod drawn from the Order of Dionysis & Paul, a religious order within the Holy Celtic Church.

2   Matthew. 6:33

Appendix 2

Early References

The following references are supplied to illustrate the distinct presence that Christianity had in Roman Britain from a very early period. It is clear from the many references made by senior and influential members of the pre-Augustinian Church, such as are quoted below, that there was not only a Christian presence in Britain but that the British Church played an active role in the life of the Church at large. It is reasonable to assume that although Britain was not a 'Christian state' in the modern sense of the word, Christian communities undoubtedly existed, and that they shared in the various fortunes of Roman and post-Roman Britain, especially during the fifth and sixth centuries. Good arguments have been put forth[1] elsewhere to demonstrate that until monasticism was introduced to these islands in the fifth century, such communities were generally urban communities, and it was these urban communities that constituted the ancient British Church.

Tertullian of Carthage (c. 160 - c. 225): Converted from paganism and became one of the most influential Christian thinkers of his day. Although never popular with Church leaders he was nonetheless instrumental in shaping Christianity. He wrote a great number of works of which thirty-one are extant. His legacy, which rested not only in his writings but in his rhetorical style, gave Christians the means to engage in debate with hostile representatives of established religion on their own ground and defeat them. In his work entitled: *An Answer to the Jews,* Tertullain states(emphasis added):

> "For upon whom else have the universal nations believed but upon Christ who is already come? For whom have the nations believed — Parthians, Medes, Elamites,

---

1   See Bibliography & Early References

and they who inhabit Mesopotamia, Armenia, Phrygia, Cappadocia, and they who dwell in Pontus, and Asia, and Pamphylia, tarriers in Egypt, and inhabiters of the region of Africa which is beyond Cyrene, Romans and sojourners, yes, and in Jersualem Jews, and all other nations; as for instance, by this time, the varied races of the Gaetulians, and the manifold confines of the Moors, all the limits of the Spains, and the diverse nations of the Gauls, *and the haunts of the Britons, inaccessible to the Romans,* but subjugated to Christ."

A Roberts & J. Donaldson, Edit. *The ante-Nicene Fathers,* Vol. III. P. 158 (Wm. B. Eerdmans Pub. Co., Grand Rapids, Michigan, 1963)

Origen of Alexandria (185 - 254), possibly the most learned and influential theologian of his time. Origen's commentaries, sermons and homilies have been an important source of inspiration to Christian luminaries, saints and theologians for centuries. His homilies constitute 'the oldest body of Christian sermons in existence.'[2] In his *Homilies on Luke,* Origen makes the following statement (emphasis added):

"The power of the Lord and Saviour *is with those who are in Britain,* separated from our world, and with those who are in Mauretania, and with everyone under the sun who has believed in his name."

Homilies on Luke, Joseph T. Lienhard S.J. Trans., (The Fathers of the Church Vol 94, Catholic University of America Press, 1996) Homily 6, Cap. 9, p. 27

Eusebius (c. 260 - c. 340 AD) was bishop of Caesarea from c. 315. He is considered by many to be the 'father of Church history' and the world owes him a debt of gratitude for the immense range of material he compiled concerning the early Church. His

2   Scheck, Thomas, Trans. *Origen: Homilies 1 - 14 on Ezekiel* The Newman Press, New York/Mahwah, NJ 2010, p. 2.

Appendices

Demonstratio Evangelica, (Proof of the Gospels) is one of the great classics of the Christian Church, and it is in this work that the following quotation is to be found (emphasis added):

"...But to preach to all the name of Jesus, to teach about His marvellous deeds in country and town, that some of them should take possession of the Roman Empire, and the Queen of Cities itself, and others the Persian, others the Armenian, that others should go to the Parthian race, and yet others to the Scythian, that some already should have reached the very ends of the world, should have reached the land of the Indians, and some have *crossed the ocean and reached the Isles of Britain...*"

The Proof of the Gospel. W. J. Ferrar, trans: (Grand Rapids, Michigan, Baker Book House Co., 1981.) First published *Demonstratio Evangelica* 1920, by S.P.C.K., Book 3, ch. 5, cap. 112 (d), p. 130.

Gildas (c. 500-570): A British monk, who lived in the first half of the sixth century. His work *De Excidio Brittaniae* is the earliest known record of the tumultuous decades of post-Roman Britain and the invasion of the Saxons. Below are excerpts from this work concerning the Christian presence in Britain:

"8. Meanwhile, to the island stiff with frost and cold, and in a far distant corner of the earth, remote from the visible sun, He, the true sun, even Christ, first yields His rays, I mean His precepts. He spread, not only from the temporal firmament, but from the highest arc of heaven beyond all times, His bright gleam to the whole world in the latest days, as we know, of Tiberius Caesar. *At that time the religion of Christ was propagated without any hindrance, because the emperor, contrary to the will of the senate, threatened with death informers against soldiers of that same religion.*

"9. God, therefore, as willing that all men should be saved, magnified his mercy unto us, and called sinners no less than those who regarded themselves righteous. He of His own free gift in the above mentioned time of persecution, as we conclude, lest Britain should be completely enveloped in the thick darkness of black night, kindled for us bright lamps of holy martyrs. The graves where their bodies lie, and the places of their suffering, had they not, very many of them, been taken from us the citizens on account of our numerous crimes, through the disastrous division caused by the barbarians, would at the present time inspire the minds of those who gazed at them with a far from feeble glow of divine love. I speak of Saint Alban of Verulam, Aaron and Julius, citizens of Caerleon, and the rest of both sexes in different places, who stood firm with lofty nobleness of mind in Christ's battle.

"12. Thus when ten years of the violence referred to had scarcely passed, and when the abominable edicts were disappearing through the death of their authors, all the soldiers of Christ, with gladsome eyes, as if after a wintry and long night, take in the calm and the serene light of the celestial region. They repaired the churches, ruined to the ground; they found, constructed, and completed basilicae in honour of the holy martyrs, and set them forth in many places as emblems of victory; they celebrate feast days; the sacred offices they perform with clean heart and lip; all exult as children cherished in the bosom of their mother, the Church."

Hugh Williams, *Gildas De Excidio Brittanniae*, Cap. 8 - 12, pp. 21-31, (Facsimilie edition Llanerch Press, Cribyn, Lampeter, 2006. Originally published by David Nutt 1901)

The Venerable Bede (c. 673 - c. 735) Bede was a monk of the united Northumbrian monasteries of Wearmouth and Jarrow. He wrote a great deal on scientific subjects of his time, demonstrating a great breadth of learning, and many of his commentaries on scripture were read publicly in churches. However, it is his work

The Ecclesiastical History of the English People that earned him the title "The Father of English History". In chapter six of this work the following quotation may be found (emphasis added):

> "Diocletian in the East and Maximian Herculius in the West, commanded the churches to be destroyed and the Christians to be slain. This persecution was the tenth since the reign of Nero, and was more lasting and bloody than all the others before it; for it was carried out incessantly for the space of ten years, with burning of churches, outlawing of innocent persons, and the slaughter of martyrs. *At length, it reached Britain also, and many persons, with the constancy of martyrs, died in the confession of their faith.*"

Bede, *The Ecclesiastical History of the English Nation*, Everymans Library, J.M. Dent & Sons. London., p.10-11

Appendix 3

Lines of Succession of the Holy Celtic Church

THE EASTERN LINE VIA THE HOLY SYRIAN ORTHODOX CHURCH

Mar Ignatius Peter III Patriarch of Antioch consecrated on the second of June 1886 (OS) **Mar Julius** (Julius Ferrette) who then consecrated in 1874, **Mar Pelagius** (Richard William Morgan) who consecrated in 1889 **Mar Theophilus** (Charles Isaac Stevens) who consecrated in 1890 **Mar Andries** (Albert Maclagan) who consecrated in 1922 **Mar Jacobus II** (Charles Monzanie Heard) who consecrated in 1943 **Mar Basilius Abdulah II** (Dr Bernard Crow) who consecrated in 1944 **Hugh George De Willmott-Newman (Mar Georgius)**. On the twenty-seventh of May 1950 Mar Georgius consecrated **Abp Harold Percival Nicholson.**

THE LINE FROM THE CHURCH OF ENGLAND

In 1787 Bp John Moore consecrated for the Church in America and as Bishop of Pennsylvania, William White, who in 1832 consecrated Bp John Henry Hopkins, who consecrated in 1886 Bp George David Cumins, who became the first presiding Bishop of the Reformed Episcopal Church. Bp Cumins consecrated in 1876 Bp William Rufus Nicholson. The line continues through Bp Alfred Spencer Richardson, Bp James Martin, Bp Benjamin Harris, who consecrated in 1944 **Bp Charles Leslie Saul,** who then consecrated in 1946 **Abp Hugh George De Willmott-Newman,** who consecrated on the twenty-seventh of May 1950 **Abp Harold Percival Nicholson.**

THE ROMAN LINE VIA THE OLD CATHOLIC CHURCH OF HOLLAND

On the twelfth of November 1668 Cardinal Antonio Barberini of the Roman Catholic Church consecrated Bp Charles Maurice Letellier, who later consecrated Bp Jaques Benigne Bossuet. The line continues from Bp Bossuet through Bp Jamed Goyen de Matignon, Bp Dominic Marie Varlet, Bp Petrus Johannes Meindaerts. Through an irreconcilable dispute the Dutch Church separated from Roman Jurisdiction. The Old Catholic bishops succeeding from the Roman Line are as follows: Abp Meindaerts consecrated on the eleventh of July 1745 Bp Johannes van Stiphout, who later consecrated Abp Gualterus Michael Nieuwenhuizen. The line continues through Abp Johannes

Broekman, Abp Johannes Jacobus van Rhjin, Bp Gijsbertus Cornelius de Jong, Abp Willibrordus van Os, Abp Johannes Bon, Abp Johannes van Santen, Bp Hermanus Gustave Hiejkamp, Bp Casparus Johannes Rinkel, Abp Gerardus Gul, who consecrated on the twenty-eighth of April 1908 for the Church in Britain, Bp Arnold Harris Mathew. The line continues through Frederick Samuel Willoughby, **Abp James Bartholemew Banks**, who consecrated:

Bp Sidney Ernest Paget Needham
Who then consecrated 4th January 1945

Abp Hugh George De Willmott Newman
Who then consecrated 27th May 1950

Abp Harold Percival Nicholson
Who then consecrated 14th April 1952

Abp Philip Charles Stuart Singer
Who then consecrated 14th November 1954

Abp Charles Brearly
Who then consecrated 26th March 1967

Abp Anthony Walter John Williams
Who then consecrated 20th May 1979

Abp Illtyd Thomas
Who then consecrated 9th October 1983

Abp Morris Frank Saville
Who then consecrated 22nd May 1988

Bp Allan Armstrong
Who on twenty-first of September 1991 was installed as the new Archbishop and Primate of the Holy Celtic Church

Appendix 4

List of Members Past & Present

The following list is of people who are described as members in each of the three volumes of Order Records. To the best of my knowledge they were *bona-fide* initiated members. I may have omitted a few, or even included one or two that should not be included, especially from the earlier years. If I have, then I ask for your forgiveness, it is not intentional.

(Vol 1) Wilf Reed; Ken Garland; Anne Spering; Gerard Decieco; Gerald Wills; William Seeney; Dennis Green; Peter Green; Colin Atkins; William Newman Norton; Winifred Burghles; Morris Saville; Beatrice Harvey; John Roseweir; Joseph Brow; Sister Iris; John Hopes; Miss Osborn; S. McClanerhan; Ruby Gowan; Enid Styles; E. Keyes; Mrs Manell; D. Keyes; Derek Tanner; William Antony Fields.

(Vol II) Mr & Mrs Thomas Pruewitt; Stephen Gunstone; Lesley Ann Gunstone; Christine Saville; Michael Startup; Allan Armstrong; Pat Moffatt; Christopher Scott-Strother; Paul Baker; Martin Bithrey; Alan Bain: Colin Richens; Eric Eades; Peter Hill; Andrew McDougall; Trevor Gardiner; Charles Hassler; Janet Tyler; Mary Macdonald.

(Vol III) Lillian Rimmer (née Kitusa); Tim Sheppard; Lawson Povey; Tina Michael; Diana Hughes; Sheila Murison; Wayne Armstrong; Saul Haines; Howard Bult; Janet Powell; Barry Bendell; Yvonne Robshaw; David Friese-Green; Julie Swarbrick; Peter Graham; Austin Jones; Catherine Thompson; Bjorn Almgren; Hilary Weston; Royden Harrill; Sara Maggs; Raymond Hall.

Appendix 5

Concerning the Name

THE ORDER OF DIONYSIS & PAUL

The name 'The Order of Dionysis & Paul' was first suggested as the name of the Order by the late Mar Dionysis (Dennis Green) the founder of the Order. The earliest clear reference to it is found in his Last Will & Testament, dated the 23rd August 1968. Dennis authorised the name of the Order to: "be changed to the "*Order of Dionysis & Paul the Apostle*" in due season." The change was delayed as other circumstances prevailed, but in November 1982 the Order changed its name, omitting '*the Apostle*' as being a tautology.

This name has a very special significance. The name "*Dionysis*" refers to St Paul's Athenian convert, Dionysis the Areopagite, (see Acts 17:34) and alludes to the wisdom of the Graeco-Roman world being absorbed into the new world order of Christianity. The name "*Paul the Apostle*", alludes to the spiritual teachings of the Lord Jesus Christ being introduced to the Graeco-Roman world — the world of the Gentile.

Thus, the title, *The Order of Dionysis & Paul*, alludes to the fusion of the ancient traditions of the classical world being sublimated, absorbed and shaped into the teachings of the Lord Jesus Christ. It is on these terms that the name is understood by the Order, and it is on these terms it is applied.

The Author

Fr Allan Armstrong, also known as Brother Marcus, has been a member of the Order of Dionysis & Paul since 1976. He succeeded Mar Francis as Prior General in 1991. A position he still holds.

He has devoted his life to developing a greater understanding of the spiritual life and the path of spiritual perfection. His research interests reflect this in his study of comparative religion; spiritual disciplines including prayer & meditation; liturgical studies; spiritual healing methods and mysticism.

Apart from his Order duties and bringing up a family, Allan is the author of *Tales of Brother Marcus, I & II*; *The Secret Garden of the Soul*; *Notes on Meditation*; *Aspects of the Spiritual life*; *Spiritualise Your Life*; and has written introductions to Frederic de Portal's *Symbolic Colours*; G.B. Scaramelli's *Handbook of Mystical Philosophy*; E.A. Wallis Budge's translation of *The Paradise of the Fathers*; C.E. Rolt's translation of *Dionysis on the Divine Names*; Dudley Wright's *Prayer*; Ruysbroeck's *The Adornment of the Spiritual Marriage*, and the English translation of Brianchaninov's *On the Prayer of Jesus*.

Allan currently lives in Wiltshire with his family.

CONTACT DETAILS

If you wish to contact the author
please write via the publisher:

ip@imagier.co.uk

To learn a little more about his vocational work,
please visit:

http://ecclesiasticaceltica.org/

Imagier Publishing is based in the UK and
publishes booksconcerning Christian esoteric
thought and spirituality. To learn more see:

http://www.imagier.co.uk/